Quick fixes for kids' Parties

For Johanna and Jasmine

howtobooks

Please send for a free copy of the latest catalogue to:
How To Books, 3 Newtec Place, Magdalen Road, Oxford OX4 1RE United Kingdom
email: info@howtobooks.co.uk
http://www.howtobooks.co.uk

Quick Fixes for Kids' Parties

Great fun ideas for giving kids' parties

Tommy Donbavand

howtobooks

Published by How To Books Ltd,
3 Newtec Place, Magdalen Road,
Oxford OX4 1RE. United Kingdom.
Tel: (01865) 793806. Fax: (01865) 248780
email: info@howtobooks.co.uk
http://www.howtobooks.co.uk

First published 2002

British Library Cataloguing in Publication Data.
A catalogue record for this book is available from the British Library.

Edited by Diana Brueton
Cover design by Baseline Arts Ltd, Oxford
Cartoons © Colin Shelbourn, www.shelbourn.com

Produced for How To Books by Deer Park Productions
Typeset and design by Baseline Arts Ltd, Oxford
Printed and bound in Great Britain

NOTE: The material contained in this book is set out in good faith for general
guidance and no liability can be accepted for loss or expense incurred as a
result of relying in particular circumstances on statements made in this book.
Laws and regulations are complex and liable to change, and readers should
check the current position with the relevant authorities before making
personal arrangements.

Contents

SCIENCE LAB 104

Bunsen burners at the ready for an experimental party where only the craziest scientists are invited!

SKOOLZ OWT! 109

Hey kids – leave those teachers alone! Had enough of school? Fight back with this crazy classroom chaos!

SUPERHEROES 113

Is it a bird? Is it a plane? No, it's a superhero party, so wear your underpants on the outside, and fly by!

TOON TIME 118

Run as fast as Speedy Gonzalez to a party where you can eat like Taz and have more laughs than Daffy Duck!

WHO WANTS TO BE A MILLIONAIRE? 123

Phone your friends and invite them to this party based on the popular TV quiz show!

About the Author

I was born in Liverpool, but don't know any of The Beatles. After being a total swot at school I trained as a classical actor and then, obviously, became a clown by the name of *Wobblebottom*, and toured the country wearing a red nose and scaring babies.

I entertained kids on board a Ukrainian cruise liner for four years (I'm the only person I know who can call Bingo in Russian), then headed back to dry land to play the Clearlake MC in the musical *Buddy* in London's West End. Eight years later, the producers noticed I was still there and closed the show to stop me having any more fun.

Nowadays, I write books of games, activities and party themes – including *Quick Fixes For Bored Kids*, *More Quick Fixes For Bored Kids* and *Boredom Busters* – and try to think of inventive things to do with toilet roll tubes. My neighbours think I'm weird.

With my business partner, Johanna Ewens, I have also started Fancy Pants Parties, which can devise and run kids' parties to people's own specifications. For more information, click on *www.fancypantsparties.com*

I would be grateful if someone reading this could e-mail me with the correct time, as my watch has stopped.

Tommy Donbavand

Preface

Part one: The Rules

**Organising a kids' party is great fun!
No, wait! Come back! I'll explain...**

How many times have you dropped your kids off at a party, only to witness chaos as soon as the door is opened?

Two kids are swinging from the light fittings; another pair are tearing up the carpet and the rest are deeply engrossed in a who-can-stuff-the-most-hamsters-into-your-mouth contest.

It needn't be like that.

The only reason that kids' parties dissolve into little sessions of anarchy is boredom - and that, dear parent, is all down to you.

'But, I tried so hard!', I hear you cry. Yes, you probably did: lots of crisps, a big cake, and plenty of balloons.

The thing is, you broke the number one rule of kids' parties. The rule that you must obey at all costs, unless you want your house destroyed by a legion of little monsters...

1) NEVER, EVER PLAY MUSICAL CHAIRS! Here's a secret: kids hate the game. Even if they once enjoyed it, they've played it at every birthday, Christmas and end of term party they've ever been to. Plus, you're the one who has to cope with a dozen or more bored kids careering round the edges of the room while two determined finalists battle it out for that final seat.

That leads me nicely to rule number two:

2) NEVER PLAY GAMES THAT INVOLVE KIDS BEING 'OUT' If you play games that keep all the kids involved from start to finish, you've got their attention - and when you've got their attention, they aren't scratching their name into the varnish of your dining table. Simple, really.

Here are a few more tried and tested party laws:

3) GET RID OF THE PARENTS Aside from the ones that are there to help, parents get in the way. Plus, their kids won't really start to enjoy themselves until their figure of authority has gone.

4) GIVE EACH KID A NAME STICKER Not only will you remember who everyone is, they also help quieter children to break the ice, and you can write everything from parents' mobile numbers to special dietary requirements on them, thus avoiding needless stress.

5) ALWAYS HAVE A PARTY THEME It's the 21st century. A few party poppers and re-lighting candles just don't do it anymore. A party theme gets the kids excited from the moment they receive their invitation, and gives you something to do on the big day as they start to arrive. The early kids can make extra bits of costume or help with last minute decorations while they're waiting for their friends to turn up.

Then, run the party in this order:

6) GAMES – FOOD – PRESENTS Always leave the opening of the presents to the end of the party to avoid gifts getting broken or lost in the fun. And if you get the kids running wild after they've had food, you're just asking for trouble!

Part Two: The Themes

This book contains 25 great themes to help your party go with a bang! There are kids' favourites such as *Harry Potter* and *Winnie The Pooh*, plus a handful of more obscure ideas, like *Party Political* and *Highland Games*. Something for every occasion.

Don't, however, treat the themes as set in stone. You know your kids far better than I do, so feel free to add your own touches, and leave out others. Flick through the book and see what you can use; maybe a game from *Mars Attacks* could be adapted for a *Desert Island* party? Or a recipe idea from *Rainbow* would fit in with your *Hollywood* theme?

Part Three: Final Words

I'd love to know how you get on with these party themes. When you use one of them, it would be great if you could e-mail me at *parties@wobblebottom.com* and tell me how it went. You can also use that address to send scanned photos of the party in progress, or to ask any questions about the themes.

Finally, log on to my web site – *www.wobblebottom.com* – for info on my other books, extra games and activities, or just to say hello.

Don't be bored!
Tommy Donbavand

Backwards

**A back to front party which finishes well,
and then starts even better!**

Invitations

Reverse writing is the way to invite guests to a backwards party, and the best thing is – it's easy to do!

Use a soft pencil to write your invitation on a sheet of tracing paper. Then, turn the sheet over, and lay it onto a piece of white A4 paper, and trace over the lettering again. Remove the tracing paper, and the soft pencil should have left a faint, backwards outline on the sheet below it. Go over this outline with a felt tip pen and your writing is reversed!

To read their invites, your guests will have to hold the paper up to a mirror!

Decoration

Turn your party room inside out, back to front and upside down! Anything you can alter so that it looks the wrong way will give the right impression!

Turn chairs around so that they face the wall. Take photographs of the backs of your family's heads, and put them in frames around the room. Instead of ornaments, stand bottles of ketchup, and salt & pepper shakers along the mantelpiece, and why not copy the spines of your books onto a sheet of card and tape it over the TV screen?

This is where you can really let your imagination run riot – the sillier, the better!

Costumes

On your backwards invites, tell guests to come to the party dressed the wrong way around! They can wear their shirts and trousers back to front, twist a baseball cap so that it's facing the wrong way, and even make cardboard shoes to tie to their heels!

How many other backwards clothing ideas can you think of? Glasses on the back of your head? Gloves on your feet? Or even underwear on the outside?

Superman would fit right in!

Games

Even the games run the wrong way at this party! Award points before you start each activity, and take them away from the winners at the end!

BACKTRACKIN'. You'll need access to a turntable to create the music for this game or, if you have a CD player with a line-out function, you could load the songs onto your computer, and use Windows Sound Recorder to change it around.

Split your guests into two teams, and give each group a pen and piece of paper. Now, play snippets of pop songs which are running backwards, and see if the players can guess what they are.

Give clues to each song title by showing pictures of the artist, or giving your guests a choice of three possibilities.

After each back to front song, give the kids a few seconds to confer, then write down their answer.

They'll be tapping their hands and clicking their toes!

REVERSE! A wrong way around game filled to the brim with giggles!

Make a set of cards that give everyday tasks, such as eating breakfast, getting up, or ironing clothes.

Choose one player at a time, show them a card at random, and they then have one minute to act out the activity – backwards!

For example, if they were getting up, they could start by pretending to get undressed, dirty their teeth, put on their pyjamas, climb into bed, and fall asleep. The other players would then have to guess what the activity was supposed to be! Keep playing until everyone has tried their hand at a mixed up mime.

For even more fun, add two person activities such as delivering a wardrobe, or buying a box of cornflakes.

Barmy and backwards!

WRAP THE PARCEL. I tend to steer clear of traditional party games, as kids have played them over and over again – but this was too good to miss!

Players sit in a circle, with one kid holding a prize. In the centre of the circle lie several sheets of wrapping paper.

When the game starts, the guests pass the prize around from one person to the next in complete silence. After a while, play a music CD – this is the cue for the person currently holding the prize to grab a sheet of paper, and wrap the gift inside it! Stop the music, and the partially wrapped prize is passed around the circle again!

Keep playing until all of the wrapping paper has been used up. The winner is the person to add the final sheet. They get to keep the prize – and all the paper!

Food

Can food be backwards? Eating the wrong way around sounds like a messy business – but try these twisted treats that'll have your guests rubbing their backs with satisfaction!

SILLY SANDWICHES! Why not serve sandwiches with the fillings on the outside? Put a piece of bread in between two slices of ham, or slide a cracker into the middle of a couple of cheese slices!

This is one party where jam sandwiches would be best forgotten!

CRAZY CUTLERY. Not so much a food idea, but a way to serve it! Try eating idiotic ice cream with a knife and fork, or hand out glasses of cake for your guests to enjoy!

Party Bags

As the party comes to an end (or should that be a start?), hand out party bags with the gifts on the outside!

Tape pens, pencils and toys to the outside of your gift bags, and leave the inside completely empty.

You'll have them coming back for more! Or is that forward for less? Or should it be...

Bunfight at the OK Corral

Follow the trail to the old west as a posse of cowboy kids enjoy a party at high noon!

Invitations

You'll need a fistful of party invites to send out to your guests - each of them a wanted poster for a dangerous baddie!

Design your wanted poster on a computer, using a picture of the birthday child as the infamous bad guy! Give them a nasty sounding name, such as Four Finger Freddie or Jailbird Jasmine – and offer a reward of $1,000 for their capture.

Make sure to add the date and time for each of your new deputies to get together, reminding them to come along in cowboy and cowgirl outfits.

Print your wanted posters onto off-white paper, and hand them out to your guests.

The bad guy's days are numbered!

Decoration

Hang a sign over your front door saying, 'Birthday Gulch' to show your guests that they have arrived. If you have a long hallway, make cardboard shop signs to hang on the walls for such buildings as the jail, the bath-house, and sheriff's office. Over the door to your party room, hang a sign saying 'Saloon'.

Cut two swing door shapes with small flaps on the outside, and tape them to the doorway of your party room. They should swing closed behind anyone who enters providing they aren't treated too roughly!

Inside the room, set up a decorator's pasting table as a long bar with bottles of soft drinks along it. Add a card table with a deck spread out as a game of poker in progress, and you could even cover a few buckets in gold foil and stand them around as spittoons!

Cover the walls with more wanted posters, and play a tape of honky-tonk piano music. Your saloon is open for business!

Costumes

Your guests should all come dressed as characters from the Wild West – cowboys and cowgirls. Here are a few ways in which they can add to their costumes, which you could run as a warm-up activity while everyone arrives.

Make sheriffs' badges by cutting star shapes from card (or, cut out two triangles, and staple one upside down onto the other). Cover the star with foil, and tape a safety pin to the back.

You can make a set of spurs in the same way, only instead of using a safety pin, attach two pipe cleaners to fasten the stars around the back of your guests' shoes, tying them to the shoelaces at the front.

Games

I'm not a particular fan of kids playing with guns, although some of your guests are bound to bring cap pistols with them as part of their costumes.

Here are a few gun-free games to show your guests how the West can be won:

HIGH NOON. A target practice game where the most dangerous weapon is an inflated balloon!

Paint six toilet roll tubes to look like empty cans (you could copy the designs from cans of soft drink).

Line them up on the edge of a table, side by side, and remove any breakables from the area.

Now, give each guest two balloons, and tell them to inflate them, but not to tie knots in them, just hold a balloon in each hand, down at their sides.

In turn, your balloon slingers step up to the line of cans, and stop a few metres away. When you shout 'Draw!', they must lift both balloons up from their sides, and release them at the same time to fire them at the targets! The aim is to see how many of the cans they can knock over with the flying balloons. Make a note of each guest's score, then reset the cans, and invite the next sharp shooter to take a turn.

HORSESHOE SHUFFLE! A silly shoe sharing game that's sure to raise some laughs.

Cut out two horseshoe shapes from card for each guest, then ask them to take off their shoes, and tape a horseshoe to the bottom of each. When they have done this, throw all the shoes into a big pile in the middle of the room.

Tell your guests to lie around the edges of the room with their eyes closed, as though they were asleep on the prairie. While they aren't looking, mix the shoe pile up even more!

Your cowherds' dreams are shattered by rustlers trying to steal their livestock! When this happens (you could make a sound like a cow to warn them!), the cowboys must mount their horses to save the herd.

They do this by shuffling into the centre of the room on their bottoms, and finding a pair of shoes to put on. It doesn't have to be their own pair; the kids will soon dissolve into giggles as they try to squeeze their feet into shoes several sizes too small!

When everyone has found a pair, throw all the shoes back into the room, send the cowboys back to sleep, and wait for the rustlers to strike again!

Don't have a cow, man!

BUCKIN' BRONCOS! Hats off to a simple, yet entertaining game.

Split the group into two teams, and give each team an identical baseball cap, on the top of which you have securely pinned a cardboard cutout of a rodeo rider!

Each team must choose a player to be their next Buckin' Bronco, and place the hat on their head (they are not allowed to adjust the size of the cap).

Play some country and western music to start the game, and your riders come racing out into the centre of the room. The aim is for each player to shake themselves about so much that they dismount their rider (the hat falls off!). They are not allowed to touch the cap with their hands, or hit it against the wall or furniture. The rider must be thrown by sheer movement alone. Get all the other players to cheer their team mate along.

When one rider finally hits the ground, stop the music, and award that bronco's team a point. The hats are passed on to two more horses, and the broncos buck again!

Food

Out on the trail, there isn't much opportunity to cook fancy food. Cowboy tuck is plain, simple and filling!

Try these recipes from the ranch:

BANGERS & BEANS. Cook as many low-fat sausages as your grill can handle, and mix them in with a big bowl of beans. Your hungry cowherds can help themselves to ladles of this filling feast – ideally onto metal plates!

KENTUCKY RED-EYE. Not that I'm suggesting you serve whiskey to your party guests, but you can get the same Wild West effect by pouring cola from an old glass bottle (label removed in case it gives your guests ideas!) into small shot glasses. Cheers!

Party Bags

As your tired ranch hands head back to their bunks for the night, give them something to remember their day by.

Make a stencil for 'Old Ma's General Store', and paint the logo onto strong brown paper bags. Inside put a plain wanted poster for your guests to add their own photo, some balloons to practise sharp shooting with, and maybe a book about cowboys in the old west.

Then watch them mosey on out of town!

Cruising

Take to the high seas for a party packed with luxury and glamour, with absolutely no chance of seasickness!

Invitations

Any passengers wishing to board a cruise liner must be in possession of a ticket. You can make these to hand out as your invitations.

Use your computer's word processor or publishing program to design the tickets. They should be approximately 20cm by 10cm in size. Add a picture of a ship (check the clip art gallery or search online), and give your liner a name starting with MV (Motor Vessel.) A good idea is to use your birthday child's name, such as the MV Luke or MV Aoife.

Next, type in the date and time of the cruise, and where it will be sailing from (all your party details), and finally, your passenger's name.

You should be able to copy the ticket and paste it so that you have three on a page. Simply change the guest's name for each, print them off, and cut them out.

Put your tickets in envelopes with the ship's name on the top, and hand them out to your lucky passengers.

Decoration

Your front door will be transformed into the gangway. Use a large piece of wood to create a slope into the ship, taking care that it won't slip from underneath their feet and hurt them. Collect tickets as your passengers arrive.

Your party room will be the recreation deck of the liner. On one side of the room, pin lengths of blue crepe paper to the wall for the sea, and cut strips of white card to make railings (so you don't accidentally fall into it!)

Along the opposite wall, cut round porthole shapes from tin foil and stick them up in a row. Add a few deckchairs beneath them for passengers to relax and watch the waves go by (or use normal chairs, and throw towels over them.) At the end of the room, tie two lengths of rope to chairs to create the bow of the ship (the pointy end!).

Costumes

Your passengers are now on holiday, and that means they will dress ridiculously!

On their tickets, ask them to come wearing bright Hawaiian shirts, shorts, flip flops or deck shoes, and sunglasses. The louder and sillier the better!

For those of you running the party, wear crisp white shirts and dark trousers. Cut epaulettes from dark crepe paper and pin them to your shoulders to transform yourselves into the ship's entertainment officers, ready to fulfil your passengers' desires, 24 hours a day. (Sounds like a tough job? It is – I did it myself for four years!)

Games

Deck sports are enormously popular on board cruise liners, with some passengers returning cruise after cruise just to keep their trophies. Here are a couple of the games cruisers play:

DECK QUOITS. A simple game where players throw rings made of rope towards a target painted on the deck. Here's an easier to prepare party version.

Use lengths of string to create three circles on the floor: one large, one smaller inside it, and the smallest in the centre. These each represent a different score – 10 points in the centre circle, five in the next one out, and two points for the outer ring.

Next, cut rings from coloured card by drawing around a small plate, and then drawing around a saucer inside it. Cut around both lines and you have a deck quoit! Make three of one colour, and three of another.

Now the game begins. Two players step forward, and take it in turns to throw their quoits from behind a line (use more string to mark this.) When all the quoits have been thrown, the points are added up.

Each game lasts three 'ends', and the player with the highest score when the game is completed is the winner.

Keep going until everyone has had a chance to play.

SHUFFLEBOARD. Another traditional ship game that requires special equipment. Here's a simpler version!

You'll need six old CDs (you could use the free Internet trial CDs from the front of computer magazines). Draw a circle on three of the CDs to separate them from the others. Two guests are chosen to play – one taking the marked CDs, the other the plain.

The aim of this version of shuffleboard is for the players to take it in turns to slide the CDs across the floor with their fingertips, into the centre of the room. Players score ten points if they manage to get two of their discs to touch or overlap each other. The opposing player can, of course, aim to knock any touching CDs apart.

When all six discs have been used, add up the scores, and play two more ends in that game. The player with the highest score at the end, wins.

FLYING FISH. One of the greatest experiences of cruising is watching the flying fish leap out of the water as the hull cuts through the waves. Recreating this is more of an activity then a game, but is still great fun!

Print off some of the great paper aeroplane designs from *www.paperairplanes.co.uk* and stick them around the

Tommy's Tip

Ironically, avoid using the design that looks like a fish! This requires a stone to be thrown inside the model, and someone is likely to get hurt!

walls. Hand out sheets of A4 paper, and let your guests try making the different styles, and throw them around the deck as flying fish!

Food

You'll be surprised what sea air can do for an appetite! Try these examples of cruising cuisine to keep it in check:

MIDNIGHT BUFFET. Ask anyone who has ever worked on a cruise liner, and they'll tell you that the most commonly asked question is, 'What time is the midnight buffet?' Before you start to laugh, on most ships, it starts at 11.30pm!

The midnight buffet is a wonderful feast of sandwiches, fruit and cakes. Lay our your party food buffet style, and let your passengers dig in!

SUNDOWNERS. There's nothing more relaxing than sitting on the deck, watching the sun set with an ice cold drink in your hand.

Try freezing orange juice or apple juice into ice cubes, and dropping them into glasses of sparkling mineral water for a refreshing evening drink.

Party Bags

As your guests disembark at the end of their cruise, they'll be trying to sneak through customs with bags full of souvenirs!

Stencil the name of your ship onto carrier bags, and fill each one with postcards, holiday brochures and designs for flying fish. Hand them out to your guests as they head down the gangway, relaxed and ready to hit dry land.

A ship shape party!

Desert Island

**Shipwreck your guests on an island paradise
for a beach party filled with fun!**

Invitations

The best way to invite guests to this party is with a message in a bottle!

Collect a clear plastic water bottle for each guest, and remove the labels by soaking the bottles in warm, soapy water.

Take a sheet of paper and tear the edges to make it look ragged. Then, rub both sides of the paper with a cold, wet teabag which will give it a weathered look.

When the paper is dry, write your invite in pencil, roll it up, and drop it into one of the bottles. Replace the top, and your invitation is ready to be delivered.

Decoration

Cover the floor of your party room with light coloured sheets, and hold them in place with rocks and bits of wood.

Make palm trees for the walls by cutting sections of tree trunk from brown crepe paper, and the leaves from green. Build the trunk piece by piece up the wall, and divide the leaves between the wall and ceiling to make it appear that the palms are leaning over the party room.

Cut a few small seagull shapes from white card, and hang them from the ceiling with cotton – and you could even stick a shark's fin to the window to make the water look infested with danger!

Costumes

Before the party, collect as many old clothes as you can (a trip to the charity shop should provide plenty) and, when your guests have arrived, give them a few pairs of scissors, and supervise as they cut the old clothes to pieces!

They can make ragged trousers, torn shirts, and battered hats. Use pieces of string for belts or braces, and soon your party guests will look as though they have been stranded on your desert island for years!

Games

Time for some shipwrecked shenanigans! A couple of these games require props being made before the party starts, but the extra effort will be worth it.

CLOUT THE COCONUT! This game is based on the traditional piñata of South American parties. You'll need to make a small coconut piñata for each guest.

For each coconut, inflate a balloon, and rest it in the mouth of a cup or glass. Now, make a basic papier mâché mix by adding two glasses of water to one glass of flour, dip strips of newspaper into it, and cover the surface of the balloon. Add four layers in all, leaving the balloon to dry between each layer.

When it is completely dry, remove the balloon from the glass, burst it, and remove it from inside the papier mâché shell. Fill the shell with a few sweets, and seal the opening with more papier mâché.

Now, paint the coconut brown and, before it dries, roll it across a plate covered with small lengths of cotton. This will make the coconut look as though it is covered in hair.

When you have enough coconuts ready, you can play the game. Hang them, three at a time, from the ceiling, and give three of your guests shorts lengths of wood (doweling is ideal). The players have one minute to bash their respective coconuts and retrieve the goodies inside. Help any kids who don't manage to break through the papier mâché shell within the time limit.

Then it's time to hang up three more coconuts, and let three more guests clout away.

SHARK HUNTER! A game where one of your guests must spot the shark before all the swimmers are attacked!

Choose one of your guests to be the shark hunter, and ask them to leave the room for a few moments. Next choose another guest to be the shark, and make sure that everyone else knows who that person is. Then, ask the shark hunter to return.

Your party room now becomes the sea, and the guests 'swim' in it by walking around, and moving their arms in a swimming stroke. The shark also does this to hide himself from the shark hunter, who simply walks around among the swimmers.

When the shark is ready – he attacks! He does this by gently squeezing one of the swimmer's legs. That swimmer must then continue swimming while counting up to five, then scream at the top of their voice, and sink to the sea bed (drop to the floor!). All the swimmers then freeze for ten seconds while the shark hunter tries to guess who the shark is. If he guesses correctly, the game is over, and another shark and hunter are chosen, but is he is wrong, the swimmers continue swimming, and the shark chooses another victim. Any victims lying on the floor should move out of the way, in case they get trodden on!

When the shark hunter finally spots the shark, pick another hunter to leave the room, and play again!

LOOPY LIMBO. Simple and silly, but loads of laughs!

Get two of your guests to hold a broom handle at shoulder height, then line the other guests up to one side of it.

Give them a topic and an initial letter – such as countries beginning with 'B', then they have to limbo under the pole in turn, and shout out their answers (Brazil, Belgium, etc).

When they have all been under, lower the pole a few inches, give another topic, and start again. If one of the players gives an incorrect answer, or touches the ground when they limbo, they must swap with one of the pole holders.

How low can they go?

Food

Your stranded guests should have plenty of fresh fruit and vegetables available on their island – and why not try these tropical treats out on them, too?

CATCH OF THE DAY. If you can brave the shark infested waters, there are plenty of fish out there to be caught! Make a tasty tuna bake, and have plates of fish sticks available for your guests.

TREASURE TREATS. Don't just hand the food to your guests on a plate – if they really were shipwrecked, they'd have to search for their meals!

Hide sweets around your party island – among the palm leaves, under rocks, etc – and let your guests hunt them out.

Party Bags

As your guests are rescued by passing parental ships at the end of the party, give each of them a goody bag wrapped in a piece of coloured cloth, and tied to a stick! You could include some jelly fish, a coconut flavoured chocolate bar, and toys to play in the sand with the next time they visit a tropical island!

They'll leave feeling hot, hot, hot!

Fairground Fun

**Roll up! Roll up! Treat your guests to the fun of the
fair with this creative carnival chaos!**

Invitations

You always know when summer has arrived when posters for the funfair appear
around your town! Recreate one of these posters for your party invitations.

You can use clip art from your computer's word processing or publishing
program to add roller coasters, candy floss and teddy bears to the poster. Make
it look as bright and colourful as possible.

Tell your guests the location of the fair (your address), and the times it will
be open. Then, print off a copy for each guest, and hand them out. They could
pin them to their bedroom walls so that they won't forget!

Decoration

As much as you'd probably like to install a full sized waltzer in your living room,
it probably isn't going to happen! However, you can add excitement to your party
room with just a few simple materials.

Tie one end of a length of string to a pin, and the other to a pencil. Stick the pin into the middle of a piece of card, and use the string to mark out a perfect circle with the pencil (be careful not to scratch the table underneath). Now, cut out the circle, and draw spokes running out from the centre to the edges of the card.

Use the remainder of the card to cut out six identical oval shapes, and draw people inside them. Fasten these around the edge of the circle with paper fasteners, to that they hang loosely.

Finally, use a nail to hang the wheel to a doorframe, again loosely, so that it spins around. You now have a distant ferris wheel, with cars that stay upright as it turns!

You can use strips of paper to cover one wall in a complicated roller coaster track. Add cardboard trains climbing up the slopes and running down the hills.

See how many other fairground attractions you can make to fill the room; there's hotdog stands, hoop-la stalls, haunted houses – and much more!

To complete the room, set up a table at the door and hand out tickets for the rides as your guests enter.

Costumes

Our funfair takes place on a hot summer's day, so ask your guests to arrive dressed accordingly!

They can wear shorts, t-shirts, flip flops, sunglasses, and hats. Have a few brightly coloured shirts handy to brighten up any quietly coloured kids!

Games

Try your hand at these attractive attractions, but watch out for crooked Carnies – fun isn't always fair!

DODGEM CARS. Split your guests into two teams, and give each group a blindfold and a broom handle.

Inflate 12 balloons, and hang them from the ceiling with cotton above head height (you could do this before the party begins), and you're ready to play.

One player from each team must put on their blindfold, and stand against the wall with the broom handle held in their hands behind their back. This will be the rod that connects the cars to the electric current above.

When the game starts, the two blindfolded players must walk across the room, taking care not to hit any of the balloons with their pole (they've got to dodge 'em – get it!). Of course, being blindfolded, they can't see where the balloons are, so the rest of their team mates must shout out directions such as 'left', 'right' and 'forward' to help them.

Of course, the guy in charge of the dodgems always plays loud music when the cars are moving, so put on a CD to add to the confusion!

The player to reach the far wall having touched the least number of balloons wins that round, then the poles and blindfolds are passed to the next player in each team, and the cars start dodging again!

> **Tommy's Tip**
> Remove any ceiling light bulbs before you start this game!

GRAB THE GOLDFISH! A wild and wet game you'll need to play outdoors!

Prepare a few props before the party for this game: two washing up bowls of water, two empty washing up bowls (or buckets), and 30 prize goldfish.

Don't worry – we're not going to use actual goldfish – these are made by filling clear plastic sandwich bags with water, adding a thin slice of carrot, and tying the top of the bag tight. Place 15 goldfish in each empty bowl at one end of the garden, and the water-filled bowls at the other.

Keep your guests in two teams and lead them outside. Half of each team stands around the water, and half around the fish.

Now start the game! The players near the fish have to throw the bags along the garden to the players waiting at the water. They must catch the fish, break open the bags, and pour them into the bowl of water. Should they not catch a fish, and it drops to the ground, the poor creature didn't make it, and is removed from the game.

Keep playing until all the fish have been thrown (make more for a longer game), then see which team saved the most, and declare them the winners!

BLAST OFF! A version of the classic fairground stall where you have to throw ping pong balls into goldfish bowls – only much, much sillier!

Place ten plastic cups in the centre of the room, and sit the players around them in a large circle. Give each player a balloon which they should inflate – but not tie a knot in – and write their name on with a marker pen.

Then, on your count of three, the players must all release their balloons at once, to see how many of them land in one of the cups, winning that player 10 points! If you've never seen a dozen or more balloons being released at the same time – you're in for a treat!

Return the balloons to their owners to re-inflate, then play again. Keep going until everyone is out of breath!

Food

Well, you weren't expecting healthy food at the fairground, were you?

TOFFEE APPLES. My favourites – and here's a great recipe for them from my book, *Boredom Busters*:

For four toffee apples you'll need 110ml of water, 225g of sugar and, of course, four apples!

Mix the sugar and water in a bowl, and cook on full power in a microwave for five minutes. Remove the bowl and stir the mixture until all the sugar has dissolved. Return the bowl to the microwave, and cook for another 15-20 minutes until the mixture turns a golden brown.

Wash the apples and push a lollipop stick into each of them. When the mixture is ready, dip the apples into the bowl, making sure to cover them completely with the toffee.

Stand them on a plate covered with greaseproof paper to cool and harden.

ICE CREAM DREAM. It's every ice cream lover's idea of fun as you let them go topping mad!

Hand out bowls of vanilla ice cream, and provide as many different toppings as you can for your guests to add on top: hundreds and thousands, raspberry sauce, wafers, chocolate flakes... they'll be screaming for more!

Party Bags

Time for the Carnies to pack the rides away for another year, and for the fairground customers to head home stuffed with burgers and candy floss!

Send them on their way clutching coloured bags, filled with balloons, sweets and small toys.

A helter-skelter of a party!

Get Fit

**Leave those crisps and sweets alone, and run a
party full of fitness, energy and fun!**

Invitations

The invitations to this party are unique – they're printed on t-shirts!

For this you'll need a plain t-shirt for every guest (you should be able to buy them quite cheaply in bulk), and iron on transfer paper that you can print with your computer.

Design the invite in your word processor, including the name of your 'gym' (your address), the date and time of the keep fit class (the party), and the personal trainer (the birthday child). Print it off onto the transfer paper (there should be a setting in your printer software to reverse the image as you print it), and iron it onto the front of a t-shirt. Repeat for each of the guests, and send the shirts out in padded envelopes.

Decoration

Decorate your party room with posters of musclemen, and gym equipment cut out from card – weights, treadmills, exercise bikes, etc. On no account should you put any real weights or equipment in the room as your guests could very easily hurt themselves.

Provide towels for your guests to dry off after the physical games, and plenty of juice and water to keep them hydrated.

If you want to get really into it, you could set up a table near the front door, and stamp a gym membership card for your guests as they arrive (you can easily make these on a computer).

Costumes

Put a note in with the t-shirt invite asking your guests to attend the party in shorts and trainers, and to bring their new t-shirt along with them.

As they arrive, they can take it in turns to design their names on the computer, which you can then print off and iron onto the backs of their t-shirts. When these are cool, they can change into them ready for their gym session!

Games

These games are all designed to get your party guests moving around, and keeping fit. If the weather is good, consider running these games outside in the garden or local park. Who knows, they might get the exercise bug, and stay fit long after the party ends?

Make sure you check with your guests' parents and find out about any physical problems, such as asthma, that may be aggravated by these games. If any of your guests can't take part, get them to help you run things.

GETTING WARMER. A great warm-up game to get their muscles relaxed, ready to exercise.

Call out a list of movements that your guests must follow, starting with very gentle exercises, and becoming increasingly energetic. Play some music during this game, and raise the volume as the exercises become more frantic.

Here are a few suggestions:

◆ wiggle your toes
◆ tap your feet
◆ clap your hands
◆ kick your legs into the air
◆ stretch up high
◆ jump on the spot
◆ jump and wave your arms about
◆ dance like mad!

At the end of the game (the end of the song), your party guests should be slightly out of breath, and warmed up enough to play the next game.

RIOTOUS RELAY! Split the party guests into two teams, and line them up, one behind the other, at the end of the room. At the other end of the room, mark two large circles with string on the floor (or simply place two hula-hoops on the ground). Beside each of these circles place a pile of cards, each with a different exercise command, such as 'run on the spot for ten seconds', 'jump into the air 12 times', and 'touch your toes twice'.

When the game starts, the first player from each team runs into the circle, and chooses the top card from the pile. Then they must follow the command on the card while still in the circle, and run back to their team. The next player then does the same, completing the exercise on the next card.

The game continues until each player has entered the circle twice, and run back to their team. The first team to complete the relay wins.

FANTASY FOOTBALL. A game that not only exercises their bodies, but gives their imaginations a work-out, too!

Mark out a football pitch in the garden or local park – you can use large stones or the traditional pile of jumpers for goalposts.

Split your party guests into two teams, and play a game of football – except without a ball!

Yes, you read that right, the aim of the game is for both teams to imagine a ball, and follow it as they play. Explain to the players that they must play as though they have a real ball, and follow the same rules (and laws of physics!). If a ball is kicked downfield, the players at the other end must wait until it reaches them before they can kick it themselves.

Things may be a little confused at first but, before long, your party guests' imaginations will start to start to work together – although you may have to play the referee and decide whether the goalkeeper managed to stop the ball, or whether it was a goal!

Remind the teams that it's only a bit of fun, and it doesn't matter who wins, as the points are just as imaginary as the ball!

Food

Replenish that lost energy with fresh fruit and pasta, plus these tasty, and healthy treats:

DIPPY DIPS! Easy to prepare, and great to eat. Cut up lengths of carrot, celery and red and yellow peppers, and stand them together in glasses. Your local supermarket should have plenty of low-fat dips to go with them.

JUICE BOOSTER! If you have a juicer (or can borrow one for the party), you have a whole range of energy providing drinks at your disposal! Try carrot, apple, and a little ginger for loads of vitamins and minerals!

Party Bags

As your gym members head for home, give them each a kit bag with a sports drink, apple and possibly a book about their favourite activity. Fitness and fun!

Harry Potter

Hop onto the Hogwarts Express to party with everybody's favourite wizard for a spell!

Invitations

An invitation to a Harry Potter party should ideally be delivered by owl – but as this might be difficult to arrange, you can do the next best thing and replicate Harry's invitation to take his place at Hogwarts School of Witchcraft and Wizardry.

On parchment style notepaper, write each invite in green ink, inviting the guest to join you at Hogwarts to train in the magical arts. Sign the name 'Albus Dumbledore' at the bottom of each, and add 'Owl Post' to the front of the envelope.

Decoration

The journey to Hogwarts begins at King's Cross Station. Make a sign to hang over your front door saying Platform 9¾ – the secret boarding place for the Hogwarts Express.

When your guests arrive, you'll take them to the wondrous place where they can acquire their magical equipment for the party – Diagon Alley. Have one room ready with cloaks and wands (see 'costumes' below), and as many fantastic looking items as you can find: toy owls and bats, piles of old books, boxes filled with magic dust (talcum powder mixed with glitter), bags of mysterious ingredients, etc.

Split your main party room into four by making banners for each of the Hogwarts houses – Gryffindor, Ravenclaw, Hufflepuff and Slytherin. Use large sheets of paper, or tape together several sheets of A4 paper, and cover with the appropriate colours of crepe paper. Then draw and cut each of the house's crests, and stick them on. A great place to see the house designs is at *http://members.aol.com/quidditchmike/freebies.html* where you can also download some superb Harry Potter wallpaper for your PC!

Make a couple of broomsticks to hang from the ceiling by covering bamboo canes in brown crepe paper, and tying a bundle of twigs to the end. Hang a golden Snitch among them, to make it look like a Quidditch game in progress. Simply paint a table tennis ball gold, and glue a feather to either side.

Costumes

When all of your guests have arrived, take them through to the room you've created as Diagon Alley. Here they can don a cloak, and choose a wand.

To make the cloaks, simply cut open a black bin liner for each guest, trim one end so that it is slightly narrower than the other, and staple two lengths of ribbon so that the cloak can be tied in place. Never use string as this could dig into your guests' throats and hurt them.

Wands are just as easy to make. You'll need a 30cm length of doweling for each guest (and a few to spare). Paint each wand a different colour or pattern, and when dry, wrap them in pieces of dark cloth. Slip a piece of paper in with each wand describing its particular ingredients, such as 'contains dragon's breath' or 'the horn of a unicorn', etc.

When each of your trainee wizards is dressed for the occasion, it's time for them to be sorted into their houses. Take them into the main hall, and introduce them to the sorting hat.

Make a sorting hat by sewing some black material into a cone shape, and adding a few patches to age it. Also, write the names of each of the four houses on slips of paper, and drop them into a bag.

Sit each child on a stool in turn, and place the sorting hat on their head. The hat will guide their hand as they reach into the bag and pull out a slip of paper showing which house they will belong to. When they have chosen, ask them to stand beneath their new house crest.

If you want to be really true to the books, why not stitch a walkie talkie or battery operated baby monitor into the top of the hat, and have someone outside the room 'sort' each guest for you?

Try to split your guests evenly among the houses. It is possible that they will all want to belong to Gryffindor (Harry Potter's house), and none to Slytherin (the house with magicians of the dark arts), but explain that the sorting hat makes the choices, and they can swap at the end of the party if they wish.

Games

Each of the four houses will be playing for points, hoping to win the house cup at the end of term.

QUIDDITCH. No Harry Potter party would be complete without this broomstick based sport. This version is Quidditch practice, using the Quaffle only. (If you haven't read any of the Harry Potter books, and are feeling utterly confused, learn the rules of Quidditch at *http://members.aol.com/magoo0885/harry/rules.htm*).

Make three goals at either end of the room by cutting hoops from card, and attaching them to the wall with cardboard 'brackets' (the hoops should be approx. 30cm away from the wall). Inflate a red balloon (the Quaffle) so that it fits easily through each of the hoops.

Each house will play three 3-minute games against the other teams in turn (six games in all). The aim of the game is for each team to hit the Quaffle with their hands, and knock it through one of the opposing team's goals for 1 point. At the end of the game, the winning team is awarded 10 points for their house.

SPELL BOUND is a wizardly game of spell casting – wands at the ready!

Each house is given six cards showing spells from the Harry Potter books:

◆ Wingardium Leviosa – (makes an object fly)
◆ Lumos – (lights the end of your wand)
◆ Petrificus Totalus – (turns a person rigid)
◆ Sonorus – (makes your voice louder)
◆ Riddikulus – (makes bad things appear funny)
◆ Obliviate – (wipes the memory)

The person running the game also has a copy of these cards, and stands in the centre of the room as the Spell Master.

The Spell Master chooses one of his or her cards, but does not show anyone else. The houses must try to guess which spell has been picked, and nominate one of their players to step forward and cast a spell.

In turn, the wizard from each house waves their wand and shouts out the spell they think has been chosen. It doesn't matter if more than one house picks the same spell.

When all four houses have guessed, the Spell Master reveals his or her choice by revealing the card, and casting the spell on it. Any house which cast the same spell wins 10 points.

The spell master then picks another spell, and each house nominates another player to step forward. Keep the game going until everyone has had a turn at spell casting.

POTIONS CLASS. This is the class most feared by Harry and his friends, as it is taught by the unpleasant Professor Snape. This version is much friendlier, but just as messy – so be sure to spread plenty of newspaper around before you start.

Split the guests into groups of two or three, depending on how many you have. Each group will need a large plastic bowl or, if you can find them, a plastic cauldron (which you should find in party shops around Halloween time).

Each group will also need a selection of potion ingredients, which are great fun to make up:

◆ Powdered Dragons' Tooth - (bicarbonate of soda)
◆ Bats' Claws - (cloves)
◆ Chopped Snake Skin - (mixed herbs)
◆ Spiders' Blood - (red food colouring)
◆ Snake Poison - (at least 250ml of vinegar)

You can have as many extra ingredients as you can think up, but those above are the essentials. Put them in clear sandwich bags or bottles with labels for each group.

Tell the class that you are making an invisibility potion and that they must be very careful to get it right because, if it starts to bubble up, they will become invisible for ever!

Start by sprinkling the Powdered Dragons' Tooth into the cauldron, followed by a few Bats' Claws, and a drop of Spiders' Blood - all the while warning your pupils to watch for bubbles. Try to make sure that everyone gets a go at adding an indredient.

Drop some Chopped Snake Skin into the mix, then it's time to cast the spell before the final ingredient is added. Get everyone to wave their wands and chant 'Bubblus Horrificus', then pour the bottle of Snake Poison into the cauldron.

The vinegar will react with the bicarbonate of soda, causing an explosion of bubbles! Listen for the screams as your class is turned permanently invisible - you could even pretend not to be able to see them!

Food

Provide your guests with food on silver or gold paper plates, and drinks in plastic goblets as a Hogwarts welcoming banquet.

Here are a couple of other ideas to add to the fun.

BERTIE BOTTS EVERY FLAVOUR BEANS. You can actually buy these now, but it's just as easy to split normal jelly beans into separate colours and label the bowls with names such as 'Cabbage', 'Earwax', 'Dog Poo' – and let their imaginations do the rest!

BUTTERBEER is the delicious drink that Harry and his pals enjoy at The Three Broomsticks in Hogsmeade. Although there isn't an official recipe available, the Internet is packed with different versions to try out.

One such site suggests melting some vanilla ice cream in a microwave, and adding half a can of diet cola, and little cinnamon to taste. Why not give it a go?

Party Bags

As the students of Hogwarts head home for the holidays, give them each a bag made from purple material to hold their wands, and include a packet of Harry Potter trading cards, and a chocolate frog in each. Tie the bags with silver ribbon for added magical effect.

Finite Partythemum!

Henry VIII

Let them eat cake!

**Join the fun at the royal court for a
banquet of king size proportions!**

Invitations

A royal decree invites all party guests to attend this event!

On sheets of off-white paper (or, you can rub a wet tea bag on white paper
and let it dry for the same effect) announce that His Majesty King Henry VIII
commands his loyal citizens to visit the palace at the date and time of the party.

Roll these sheets up, tie them with lengths of red ribbon, and get one of your
servants to deliver them!

Decoration

Turn your living room into a castle hall by making regal looking banners to hang
from the walls. Tape together several sheets of paper, and draw a crest in the
centre. Paint the banner in bright colours, and pin it up. Repeat this process for
each of the kingdoms you currently rule over!

Complete the room with a long, impressive table in the centre. Simply cover a decorator's pasting table with purple and yellow crepe paper for an instant royal banqueting table!

Costumes

Ask your guests to come to the party wearing prince or princess costumes: girls can wear long dresses, while the boys can tuck their trousers into their socks, and wear an open necked shirt and waistcoat.

As a fun activity, let your guests make crowns as they arrive. Cut crown shapes from card beforehand, but don't fasten the ends together. Provide glitter and packets of small plastic gems to stick to the crowns with PVA glue, then staple them to the right size for each guest.

Games

You will need to use a separate room for party games so as not to upset your banqueting table or, if the weather is good, consider playing these regal riots outside:

OFF WITH HER HEAD! Henry VIII is, of course, known for his taste in wives – quantity over quality! Now your party guests can help the king get rid of his unwanted spouses with this game of excruciating executions!

Cut six torsos from sheets of stiff card – from the chest to the neck – and dress them up using bits of old material so that they look like the top bits of six Queens!

Attach cardboard flaps to the sides to enable the torsos to stand upright.

Finally, glue a clothes peg to the back of each neck with the open part at the top, and you're ready to play.

Inflate six balloons, and draw a face on each. Clip one balloon into each of the pegs, giving Henry's wives a head each.

Choose one of your guests to be the executioner, and give him his axe (cut an axe shape out of doubled over card, and tape a pin to the axe blade, reminding everyone to be careful).

Now, blindfold the executioner with a piece of material, and let him loose! He has one minute to burst all six Queens' heads. The other guests can cheer him on (remember to keep them well back; there's a pin on the end of that axe!).

When the time is up, remove the executioner's blindfold and let him see how well he has done. Then, replace any burst heads, choose another guest to wield the axe, and play again!

HUNGRY HENRY. How much grub can Henry eat at one sitting? Pile it on his plate and find out!

Provide each guest with a paper plate (you could paint them gold to make them look more regal!), and place a large pile of food in the centre of the room. Make sure to choose items which won't be ruined or stain the carpet, such as tins of soup, packets of cereal, etc.

Choose two guests to bring their plates forward and kneel by the food pile. When the game starts, they will have one minute to pile as much food on Henry's plate as they can, without it falling off!

When the time is up, make a note the number of items each guest has managed to add to their plate, and invite two new guests to play. The player with the highest number at the end of the game gets a prize!

HEY, FATTIE BUM BUM! Large it with this game of immense proportions!

You'll need some extra large dressing up clothes for this game - jogging bottoms, t-shirts, etc. All as baggy as possible. Plus, inflate as many balloons as your lungs can cope with!

To play the game, four guests are chosen, and stand around the pile of clothes. When you give the signal, they must grab a pair of trousers and a top, and put them on over their own clothes. Then they have to stuff as many inflated balloons inside these items as they can!

They'll have three minutes to push balloons up their t-shirts and down their trousers, trying to make sure they don't burst! (They should always put the baggy clothes over their own to protect their skin should one of the balloons pop.)

After three minutes has passed, stop the game, and count how many balloons each player has managed to conceal. The kid with the highest number is declared to be as fat as King Henry – then new guests are picked, and the game starts again!

Food

The theme here is messy! No cutlery is allowed; your guests must eat with their fingers as they sit down to an enormous banquet.

Serve plenty of squash to quench their thirst, and try these royal recipes for sticky fingers!

SPARE RIBS. Just about the messiest food you can give a gang of hungry kids! You'll need a steady nerve to watch them smear their faces with barbecue sauce – just make sure those gooey fingers aren't cleaned off on your curtains!

FRIED CHICKEN. Here's a tasty treat you don't even have to prepare yourself! Just head down to your local fried chicken franchise and pick up a couple of buckets of chicken wings. Just made for finger eating!

Party Bags

After Henry and his court have filled their bellies, it's time for everyone to leave. They might be too stuffed to accept a piece of birthday cake, so put it into a purple or gold gift bag, and add a few other gifts, such as a book of Kings and Queens, or a souvenir from one of the royal castles.

A party fit for a King!

Highland Games

Take the High Road and delight your guests with this collection of kilted capers!

Invitations

The only way to invite guests to an afternoon of Highland hilarity is with a sporran!

Cut two identical arch shaped pieces of card for each invite, and join them together with a 'hinge' of strong sticky tape at the top. Cover the front piece of card with some fur fabric, or crumpled brown tissue paper, and add a crest made from tin foil to complete the look.

Open the sporran up, and write your invite to compete in the games inside. Make sure to tell your guests to bring this sporran invite with them to the party.

Decoration

To transform your living room into the setting for the games, create four clan banners to display on the walls.

To make these, take four large sheets of paper (or simply tape several A4 sheets together), and cover them with red, green, blue and yellow crepe paper respectively. Use coloured marker pens to draw a check pattern onto the crepe paper, making each look like a different tartan.

Now, draw a large clan crest on another sheet of paper, colour it in, and cut it out. Stick this crest over the tartan to complete the banner. A handy web site showing the various clans' tartans and crests can be found at *www.scotclans.com*

You could also make a few sets of fake bagpipes in clan colours to place around the room. Half-fill a plastic carrier bag with balls of crumpled up newspaper, fold the bag over, and tape it up until it resembles a kidney shape. Cover the bag with crepe paper, and draw the tartan pattern on with marker pens.

Roll up pieces of thin card to make the pipes, and stick five of these to the top of the bag, tying them loosely together with string. A final, shorter pipe should dangle from the side of the bag.

Play a CD of Scottish music in the background to drown out the sound of anyone trying to play your fake bagpipes!

Costumes

In your invites, ask everyone to attend the party in long socks, t-shirts and shorts. There's only one thing missing – the kilt!

Here you have a ready made activity to get the party going with a swing. Provide each guest with a roll of crepe paper in one of the clan colours and some marker pens. Get them to copy one of the tartan patterns from the banners on the wall onto their length of paper.

When they are finished, wrap the crepe paper around their waists, fold the ends over, and pin the home-made kilts in place. Try to split the guests fairly evenly among the four clans.

Your guests should have brought their sporran invitations with them (have a few spare, just in case). Tie them loosely around your guests' hips with string, so that they dangle in front of the kilt to complete the costume!

Games

At the start of your Highland Games event, introduce the four competing clans, and explain that they will be playing for points that will be added to their team's total. The winning clan at the end of the games will receive certificates of achievement.

Let the games begin!

TOSSING THE CABER. No Highland event would be complete without this favourite from 'The Heavies' – but before you start to worry about tree trunks being thrown around indoors, here's a slightly safer version! To prepare it, you'll need an empty Smarties tube, and eight plastic cups.

Fill the Smarties tube with sand to give it some weight, and securely tape or glue the top in place. Now paint the tube brown, and give it a few markings to make it look like wood.

The plastic cups will be the targets. Paint each cup a different colour, and drop a few stones in the bottom to help keep them upright. Using a marker pen, write a score on the front of each cup – from 4 to 10 points. Place the cups at various points at one end of the room.

To play the game, each contestant in turn stands behind a mark a few metres away from the targets, and balances the 'caber' on the palm of their hand. On your command, they must launch the caber into the air, and try to land it in one of the target cups (remember to remove any breakables first!). At least part of the caber must remain in the cup to win the points.

Each player has three tosses of the caber, then any points they have scored are added to their clan's total.

WEIGHT A MINUTE. Another game that tests the strength of your Scottish superstars!

In advance, blow up at least 40 balloons, and cover the knot of each with a piece of tape. Use a marker pen to number each balloon with one of three weights – 10kg, 50kg and 100kg. You can keep these balloons in plastic bin liners in another room until it's time to play.

At the start of the game, position each clan beneath its banner, and give each player within the team a number (so that you'll have four number ones, four number twos, etc). Empty the balloons in the middle of the room, and you're ready to play.

Shout out a number that corresponds with a player from each clan. The four players with that number must rush forward, grab as many balloons as they can, and hold them in their arms (the knots are covered to stop them from cheating!).

When one minute is up, the four players must stop collecting. Add together the weights on each player's balloons, and the contestant with the highest total (the strongest contestant) wins 10 points for their clan.

Replace the balloons, stand back – and shout out another number! Keep going until each player has had a go.

STUFF THE HAGGIS! Spread plenty of newspaper and plastic bin liners around – this is going to get messy!

Fill a few large buckets or washing up bowls with a mixture of porridge oats, flour and water. Give each player a clear plastic sandwich bag, and a bag tie.

When the game starts, each player must use their hands to grab as much of the goo as they can, and fill their bag. They have one minute to stuff their haggis, and secure the top with the tie.

At the end of the game, weigh each haggis in turn, and award 10, 8 and 6 points to the three heaviest.

Best of all – now your guests don't have any excuse not to wash their hands before they eat!

Food

Be sure to provide plenty of fresh fruit and vegetables so that the competitors can keep their strength up for the games – and here are a couple of other traditional delicacies your guests might enjoy.

NEEPS AND TATTIES. This delicious mix of turnips and potatoes is easy to make. Boil 2kg of potatoes and 1kg of cubed turnips in lightly salted water until tender.

When ready, drain, add a few tablespoons of milk and a knob of butter to the vegetables, and mash together.

LORNE SAUSAGE is more difficult to make (although if you want to try, there is a great recipe at *www.rampantscotland.com/recipes/blrecipe_sliced.htm*), so check with your local butcher, or larger supermarket who should be able to provide you with some.

Party Bags

At the end of the games, present all the contestants with a bag made from tartan cloth, containing toffees, shortbread, and possibly a book on how to talk in a Scottish accent!

Fare thee well a while!

Hollywood

**Hit the silver screen as you party with
the movie stars. Lights, camera, action!**

Invitations

They say that every big movie begins with the script – so why not start your block-busting Hollywood party in the same way?

Film scripts are set out in a very specific way. Follow the example below, replacing the names and details with your party information.

> **Note:**
> INT means interior,
> and EXT is exterior.

THE HOLLYWOOD PARTY – scene 1

FADE IN:

INT. BEDROOM - DAY
Luke flicks through a book of Hollywood stars, bored!

>   LUKE
>   I really wish something
>   exciting would happen!

Suddenly, the door opens, and Luke's Mum enters.

> MUM
> Luke! Aliens have kidnapped
> your Grandma, the dog has just
> started talking, and I'm arranging
> a Hollywood party for you!

Luke jumps up.

> LUKE
> I'm having a party?
> I'm going to invite Mark!

> MUM
> Tell him that the party will
> be on the 17th from 1 to 4pm,
> and that he should come dressed
> as a character from a film.

Luke writes this down as a spaceship passes the window. His Grandma is driving!

> CUT TO:

EXT. LUKE'S HOUSE, 1pm ON THE 17th.
Mark knocks on the door. Luke's dog opens it!

> DOG
> Come in, the party's about to start!

Mark stares in amazement.

> FADE OUT:

Rewrite the invitation any way you like, and change the name of the guest for each one you print off. Deliver them in sealed envelopes to keep rival producers away!

Decoration

No Hollywood party would be complete without the famous Hollywood sign!

Cut each of the letters from a large sheet of white card, and stick them along one wall in the uneven style (if you can't remember what it looks like – check out *www.hollywoodsign.org* for a 24 hour view by web cam!).

Cover the other walls in film posters and pictures of movie stars (ask at your local video shop – they often have these to give away!).

Write the name of each guest inside a cardboard star, and stick these to any remaining spaces on the walls. You could even add paint handprints below them to create the walk of fame outside Mann's Chinese Theatre!

Complete the room with a director's chair, a cardboard megaphone (simply roll a sheet of card into a cone and tape in place), and a video camera on a tripod. You can use this camera to film the party, and play the footage back while your guests eat!

Costumes

Your screenplay invites should have asked your guests to turn up dressed as their favourite movie characters. Here are a couple of ideas to get you going:

For Anakin Skywalker, the Jedi Knight destined to become Darth Vader, wear a plain brown robe (sew up an old blanket), make a long braid from wool and pin it into your hair, and roll some fluorescent card into a tube for a lightsabre.

Woody, the hero of Toy Story, can be recreated with a cowboy hat, boots (try a pair of wellies!), a checked shirt and a crepe paper waistcoat.

Let your imagination run riot!

Games

Take one for movie madness in this selection of hilarious Hollywood games!

SCREEN TEST. Test your guests in this live action board game!

Cut 20 squares from card, number them from 1 to 20, and lay them on the floor – five across and four down. On seven of the squares, add a command such as 'No Film In Camera - back two spaces', 'Star Likes Your Script - forward three squares' and 'Critics Hate Your Movie – miss a turn'.

Split your guests into two teams, and ask them to choose one player to be their Producer. These two players both stand on square one, ready to race around the board.

Now, ask each team in turn a movie trivia question. You could use questions from a kids' film quiz book, or invent your own, such as:

◆ What kind of creature is Shrek? (An ogre)
◆ Who is Harry Potter's red-haired friend? (Ron)
◆ In Monsters Inc., what colour is Mike? (Green)

If they answer correctly, their Producer moves forward one square. If they are wrong, they move back a square (until they are back at the beginning, when they remain on square one). The aim is for each team to get their Producer to the final square (which you could mark World Premiere!), and have a successful film!

The first team to do this are the winners!

SILENT MOVIE. This one's silent, simple and silly!

Split your guests into groups of four or five, and play them a snippet from a famous video, with the sound turned down. Tell everyone to watch very closely, and remember what happens.

Then, give each team a card with a theme on, such as 'Going shopping', or 'On holiday' – something not connected with the actual scene at all.

Now, bring each group forward in turn, play the silent clip again, and giggle as the team have to ad lib the characters' voices over the top of it – keeping to the theme on their card!

Encourage quieter players join in and have a go, explaining that it's not accuracy you're after – it's just a bit of fun.

At the end of the clip, rewind the tape, call up the next team, and ad-lib all over again!

DIRECTOR'S CUT! Keep your teams of four or five together for this next game of film fun. This is where a video camera will come in handy!

Ask the groups to find a space to themselves, and rehearse a scene from one of their favourite movies – from memory!

Each player should act as one or more of the characters as the groups try to recall how the silver screen snippet goes. Chances are you'll have at least one guest in each team who will take charge and direct the piece!

Your teams have ten minutes to rehearse their scene, then they must act it out in front of everyone else. Can the other guests guess which movie it comes from?

Food

In Hollywood, meal times are used as meetings. A chance to make deals, hire stars, and even ruin careers!

At your Hollywood Party, food is nothing more than fun! Why not play back the party video, or show a favourite film as your kids eat this mixture of movie munchies?

POWER LUNCH! The ultimate in Hollywood chic! Serve orange juice, muffins and fresh fruit – and watch your guests turn from innocent kids to power mad executives!

POPCORN. No movie would be complete without it! Why not try bags of popcorn you can make in the microwave? Prepare bowls of both the sweet and salted variety – and have plenty of soft drinks on hand to wash it all down.

Party Bags

As the credits roll, hand out the end of movie shoot gifts – party bags covered with stars, into which you've dropped movie posters, postcards, and a Video Voucher: a promise that if the kids provide you with a blank video cassette, you'll copy the party tape so that they can relive their Hollywood adventure again and again.

And... cut!

Jurassic Party

**Walk with dinosaurs as your guests create
prehistoric pandemonium at the party that time forgot!**

Invitations

The time and date of this party should be set in stone – as should the rest of your invite!

Cut out a flat stone shape from card, and paint it a stone grey. Before it dries, use your finger to write 'Come To My Party' in the wet paint.

Once the message has dried, you can spread PVA glue over the rough lettering, and stick small pieces of gravel to the card to give a 3-D effect. Add the location and time of the party on the back to complete your rockin' invites!

Decoration

Your party will take place outside the family cave!

Use lengths of old wallpaper to cover the wall around the door to the room. You can pin it up with small nails to keep it place, folding the paper around the doorframe to make the mouth of the cave.

Next, give the paper some relief by screwing up sheets of newspaper, and gluing them randomly around the wall. Make a papier mâché mix by adding two glasses of water to one glass of flour, and cover these paper lumps with strips of newspaper dipped in the mix. Allow them to dry, then add a few more layers.

Finally, paint the paper grey, adding a few dabs of black to give the wall the appearance of stone. You now have your very own cave entrance!

Outside the cave, make a fake fire by cutting a circle from a plastic bin liner, and glueing stones around the edge. Wedge twigs inside the stones to form a conical shape to the fire, adding more and more until you can no longer see the bin liner through the pile. Cut flame shapes from orange crepe paper, and stick them onto more twigs. Push them into the fire so that they look as though they're the result of burning wood.

To complete the room, cut pterodactyl shapes from card (one body piece and two wings), and hang them from the ceiling with cotton. You could also make greenery from crepe paper, and have cardboard dinosaur heads peeping in on the party from beyond!

(Before anyone e-mails me – yes, I know humans and dinosaurs didn't co-exist, but we'll cheat for the benefit of your party guests!)

Costumes

Ask your guests to attend the party wearing t-shirts, shorts, and with dirty faces. Shouldn't be too difficult to arrange!

As they arrive, help them to make caveman costumes from lengths of crepe paper or, even better, pieces of fur fabric. Pin smock shapes onto your guests' t-shirts, and cut bone shapes to dangle around their necks with string.

Your guests should also remove their shoes and socks for the duration of the party – so make certain that there are no sharp objects around the floor.

Games

It's prehistoric playtime! Have some spare lengths of crepe paper handy for occasional rips and tears in your guests' costumes – the age of dinosaurs wasn't kind to fashion victims!

GOING CLUBBING. Today, making friends often involves some kind of club. Back in pre-history, things were much the same!

Sit your guests in a circle around the fire (this is a good opportunity to remind them that you have made a fake fire, and never to play with the real thing), and blow up a long balloon to act as a club.

Your cave kids should cross their legs, close their eyes, and hold their hands in their laps with the palms facing up.

Wander around the circle in silence, reminding your guests not to open their eyes. Eventually, choose one of them, gently place the club into their upturned hands, and keep on circling the group.

After a few seconds, shout 'Go clubbing!'. The player with the club must quickly choose the person either to their left or their right, and hit them on the head with the balloon. Both kids then jump up, and chase around the circle – clubbing all the while – while the rest of group open their eyes and chant 'Club! Club! Club!'

When both players reach their original spaces, they sit back down, and you take possession of the club again. All players must then fall silent, close their eyes, and wait for the next clubber to be picked.

There's nothing like a good bash!

DESIGN-A-SAUR! There were some pretty weird dinosaurs around when the world was young – none more so than those invented during this game!

Give each of your guests a sheet of paper, and a few pencils. Have some paper spare in case of mistakes.

Next write a selection of different jobs on cards – such as policeman, footballer, or decorator – and keep them safe.

When the game starts, give one of these cards to each guest, and they will have ten minutes to design a dinosaur that could do that job! Perhaps the Coposaurus would have a flashing blue light on its head, white gloves to direct the pterodactyl traffic, and a roar that sounded like a siren? Would the Soccersaurus have studded feet, skin like a football strip, and live in a goalpost shaped cave?

When the time is up, pin the dinosaur drawings on the wall, and see if your guests can decide which beast does which job.

Another roaring game from the Authorsaurus Rex!

EGG ON YOUR FACE! Breakfast was the best meal of a caveman's day! Huge dino eggs are really tasty, but hard to move. Play this cracking caper with your guests and find out why!

Split your guests into two groups, and give each team a nest (cover the outside of a cardboard box with twigs), and a cooking pot (another cardboard box, painted black). Blow up round balloons to be the dino eggs (the same number as the players in each team), and place them in the nests.

The aim of the game is for each team to transfer their dino eggs from the nest and into the cooking pot. However, the shells of the eggs are poisonous until they are cooked, and cannot be touched by hand.

The players must then take it in turns to grab an egg another way, and carry it along the room to drop in the pot! They could hold it between their teeth, under their arms, or even nod it along in the air. However, should an egg fall onto the floor, it is considered broken, and must be removed from the game.

Your teams line up behind their nest, and have three minutes to complete the task. When the time is up, the team with the most balloons cooking in their pot are the winners!

Food

Food is scarce in cave times (especially as your party guests are considered lunch themselves by some very scary creatures!). However, the hunter-gatherers have managed to bag these tasty morsels to fill your tribe's tummies!

PTERODACTYL WINGS. Once you've mastered the art of catching these flying dinosaurs, you must learn how to prepare, season and serve their wings. Or, you could just grab a bucket full of chicken wings from your local fast food franchise, label them as pterodactyl wings, and hope nobody notices the difference!

ROCK CAKES. With rocks just about everywhere, it makes sense to eat them. However, while they may be filling, the taste leaves a lot to be desired!

Instead, try this recipe for rock cakes from the BBC: *www.bbc.co.uk/food/recipes/db/1/T/traditionalrockcakes_6317.shtml*

Party Bags

As darkness starts to fall, your weary cave kids head back to their stone pillows and sabre-toothed tiger skin duvets.

Give them something to enjoy before they go to bed by making cloth bags from old pillow cases, and filling them with dinosaur stickers, books and toys.

Funasaurus!

Mad Hatter's Tea Party

**Follow Alice through the looking glass, and spend an
afternoon with the crazy characters in Wonderland!**

Invitations

Please don't come to my unbirthday! That's how you should start the invitation
to Wonderland. Follow on by saying that the party will not be happening at your
address, and will not be at this time, and that anyone coming should NOT dress
as a character from Lewis Carroll's famous books!

Finally, sign the invitation from Tweedledum and Tweedledee – and don't
forget to add a PS telling guests to do the opposite of everything mentioned
above!

Decoration

You can really have some fun turning your party room into Wonderland.

Start by making a three-sided mirror frame to fit around the door into the room.

Cut an ornate frame shape from card for each side, and the top of the door,
and paint it to look like wood(don't put a frame at the bottom in case anyone trips

over it). Pin these around the doorway as the magical entrance to the world beyond.

Inside the room, place a table and enough chairs for all your guests. It doesn't matter if they don't match – the Mad Hatter never did have perfect taste!

Lay the table with a mish-mash of crockery, cutlery, ladles, tea cups and, of course, a tea pot. Make it look as strange and confused as possible.

On the wall to one side of the table, stick some dense trees cut from card and covered in crepe paper. Somewhere among the branches, add the gleaming white smile of the Cheshire Cat!

On the other side, line up a row of playing card guards, watching over the Queen of Hearts' palace. Simply draw hearts and diamonds onto large sheets of white card, and staple on a head, short arms and feet!

Costumes

As you mentioned in your invitations, your guests should come to the party already dressed as a character from the books.

For girls, wear a pale blue dress, long white socks and, of course, an Alice band in the hair to look like our heroine.

Boys can wear a top hat made from black card, and a suit jacket or school blazer with a cravat for the Mad Hatter himself (don't worry if there's more than one), or stuff a pillow up a school jumper and wear a cap to come as Tweedledum or Tweedledee!

Games

The games in Wonderland are just about as silly as anything else! Use another room so as not to disturb the tea table, or play these games outside in the garden.

DUNK THE DORMOUSE! The Mad Hatter is famed for his desire to squeeze the poor Dormouse into the teapot. Well, now's his chance – and everyone else can help!

For the game you'll need a soft toy mouse (or you could make one by stuffing an old sock and adding whiskers and a tail), a large teapot, and two cups. Make the teapot by rolling a sheet of card into a tube, and sticking in a cardboard handle and spout. Tape it down onto the cover of a large book to give it some stability. The teacups are made in the same way, and you can cut circles of card for saucers.

To play, line your party guests up at one end of the room, and place the teapot a few metres away with a cup on either side. Each player has three tries to throw the mouse into the teapot. They get 10 points if they manage to do this, but 5 unpoints (i.e. 5 points are taken away) if they land the mouse in one of the cups.

Many of the players will end up with a score in unpoints – but that's OK. It's just a bit of Mad Hatter fun!

TWEEDLE TWODDLE! A silly and simple game that will have your guests in fits of giggles.

Ask each of your guests to find a partner, and stand facing them. Now, they should decide which one of each pair should be Tweedledum, and which Tweedledee.

When they have chosen, shout out one of these names. Whichever name you call is now the leader of each pair, and should move out of the spot. Their partner must copy their moves exactly!

After a while, call out the other name – and the game swaps over. Now the other twin is the leader, and must be followed.

Keep shouting out the names, getting faster and faster as the game progresses. Things will get more and more confused, until everyone has to stop for a rest and a good laugh!

CHEESY CHESHIRE CAT. A chuckle filled game where a straight face is needed.

Players sit in a large circle, with their legs crossed. One guest is chosen to be the Cheshire Cat, and must crawl around the middle of the circle, searching for a victim!

When they have chosen, they must crawl up to that person, smile their widest smile, and say what everyone says when they grin, 'Cheeeeese!'

The player must stare the Cheshire Cat in the face, must not smile, giggle or laugh at all! If they do, they swap places with the cat, and slink off to grin at a new victim. If they manage to keep a straight face, the Cheshire Cat has to try his smile out on someone else!

Food

I'm not sure if I'd want to be a guest at the Mad Hatter's tea party with all the strange food around. You could have odd banana sandwiches containing a whole banana, or glasses of ice cold jelly!

Don't forget these daft delicacies...

THE QUEEN OF HEARTS' TARTS! Offer your guests plates of jam tarts, all sitting on plates to which stern warnings are attached; 'Anyone who eats my tarts shall 'ave their 'eads chopped right off!'

EAT ME! All the other food should be clearly labelled, 'Eat Me!' – and all the lemonade, 'Drink Me!' Plus, why not make white rabbits by adding wafer ears and sweets for eyes and nose to a scoop of vanilla ice cream?

Party Bags

Use gift bags, and stick a wide, Cheshire Cat grin on the side of each. Include a piece of cake (marked 'Eat Me!' of course), an Alice band for the girls, and a pack of playing cards for the boys.

Curiouser and curiouser!

Mars Attacks!

The Martians are here – and they're looking for fun.
Take a trip to the red planet and party!

Invitations

On 30th October 1938, Orson Welles shocked the radio listening population of the United States by announcing that the Earth was being invaded by aliens from Mars!

Of course, it was only an adaptation of the classic novel, *War Of The Worlds*, performed in the style of a series of news reports – but it was enough to cause thousands of listeners to hide in their cellars with wet towels wrapped around their heads to protect themselves from the noxious Martian gases!

Your invites to the party will be created in much the same way – but will hopefully have a very different effect!

First, write a short script from the Martian leader, commanding all Earthlings to attend a gathering at your home, on the time and date of the party. Keep it short and to the point, and make sure you include all the important information.

Now you're ready to record. Put a blank cassette into a tape player, and record your script in an eerie sounding voice. You could hold an empty metal tin up to your mouth to create a weird Martian tone as you speak. Don't worry if you make a mistake, just switch off the tape, rewind, and start again.

When you're happy with the recording, play it back to someone who hasn't read the script, to see if they can pick out the date, time and location of the party.

Finally, make a copy of the tape for each of your guests. Your kids could design a space age cover for the cassettes on a computer, with a picture of an ugly alien staring out!

Distribute the tapes to your guests, and wait for them to dutifully appear before their alien overlords!

Decoration

Mars isn't called the red planet for nothing – you'll need lots of scarlet coloured crepe paper to turn your party room into the Martian surface!

First, cover the walls with as much red crepe paper as you can. Before you pin it up, stick balls of screwed up newspaper behind it to give the walls a rocky appearance, like the inside of a crater.

Next make papier mâché rocks by dipping strips of newspaper into a mixture of two glasses of water to one glass of flour, and laying them onto inflated balloons. When the first layer is dry, stick more screwed up paper to each balloon before adding the next layer of papier mâché. Again, this will help to give the finished item a rock like texture. Cover the balloons in four layers, and paint red when dry.

Finally, make flying saucers by sticking two paper plates together face to face, and covering them with tin foil. Hang these alien spaceships from the ceiling with cotton to look like the invasion force heading for Earth. If you have an inflatable globe, you could hang it in the corner of the room as our distant home.

If you want to be really adventurous, cut two huge circles of card, glue them together with balls of paper inside to make them bulge, and push three long kitchen foil tubes into the bottom as legs. Cover the whole saucer with foil (or paint it silver), and stand it to one side of the room as a craft waiting to take off.

Your alien world is now complete!

Costumes

This is a great opportunity for a built-in activity as your guests arrive.

Provide plenty of bits and pieces such as empty boxes, sheets of paper, face paints, empty yoghurt pots, etc. As each child arrives, give them glue, scissors and string - and help them to make an alien costume to wear for the games that follow.

The great thing about aliens is that they can look any way you want - nobody has ever seen one. Let their imaginations run riot as they paint their faces green, make antennae from straws and ping pong balls, and even create extra eyes to stick to the backs of their heads!

You'll end up with the weirdest collection of party guests ever!

Games

Now for some Martian madness! Don't worry if any costumes get damaged while playing these games - they're only going to be torn off at the end of the party anyway.

POT THE PLANET! Play pool with planets with this game inspired by my favourite episode of the TV series, *Red Dwarf*!

Before the game, inflate two beach balls - one larger than the other. If you can, paint these balls once they are blown up. One green and blue as the Earth, and the other grey to represent the Moon. You may find that poster paint won't stick to the balls, so try covering them with a layer of PVA glue first.

While they are drying, you can make your black hole! You'll need a cardboard box large enough for the bigger ball to fit inside.

Remove the top flaps, and the front from the box and paint it, well... black! Let everything dry completely.

To play the game, position the black hole at one end of the room, and place the Earth in the centre. The first player is chosen, and they must stand against the opposite wall to the black hole, with the Moon at their feet.

They now have three tries to knock the Earth into the Black Hole, by kicking the Moon against it (like the cue ball in pool!). Clever players will use their first two kicks to position the Earth, and their final shot to try to knock it into the black hole.

If they manage to pot the Earth, give them a round of applause. Then reset the balls, and the next player steps forward for their turn.

It's just potty!

A SPACEMAN CAME TRAVELLING. A wacky game of words, where no-one can understand what you're saying!

Make a selection of cards, each naming a simple task, such as making a cup of tea, or taking a dog for a walk.

Each player in turn steps up, and is given a card to look at. They must not show it to any of the other players, or read what it says out loud.

They now have two minutes to explain to the rest of the guests exactly how to perform the chore they have been given – in Martian!

Yes, they have to invent a weird alien language to use while they mime whatever is on the card. It doesn't matter what it sounds like, as long as no real words are used. This might be a little difficult for younger guests to understand, so be prepared to make up some gobbledegook to demonstrate yourself!

As the alien is explaining, the other players must shout out (in English) what they think is being demonstrated. They'll only have two minutes to work it out.

When the task has been guessed, or the time is up, choose the next player, show them another card, and let *The War Of The Words* start all over again!

INVASION! This is a new version of a popular game from my book, *More Quick Fixes For Bored Kids*, which is itself adapted from a classic. It's great fun!

Players find a space in the centre of the room, and stand facing you. You will now shout out a series of commands, to which there are corresponding actions. The players must act out these moves as quickly as they can.

- ◆ Aliens Alert! (Players invent a silly salute!)
- ◆ To The Saucers! (Players mime spaceship controls!)
- ◆ Laser Attack! (Players shoot lasers from their fingers!)
- ◆ Retreat! (Players run away in a funny fashion!)

◆ Lunchtime! (Players mime gobbling up humans!)
◆ Germs! (Players drop to the floor, ill from germs!)

Run through the commands first, showing the actions, then play the game, shouting them faster and faster as the kids try to keep up.

Add any extra commands you can think of, and watch your Martians go mad!

Food

Who knows what little Martians eat at parties? Perhaps it's this...

MARTIAN MILKSHAKE. Make a delicious milkshake by mixing cherryade with ice cream and adding a few drops of red food colouring. If you can find anywhere that sells Space Dust (the sherbet like crystals that fizz on your tongue), sprinkle a little on top and serve!

GALACTIC GRUB. This is one time when you will be encouraging kids to play with their food!

Give them a piece of fruit as a base, such as an apple, orange or banana – and provide bowls of bits to add on, like cheese string, chocolate sauce, hundreds and thousands and Twiglets.

Before the guests are allowed to eat their piece of fruit, they must first transform it into an odd looking alien using the extras.

It'll be messy, but fun!

Party Bags

As your aliens return to Mars (the invasion was a failure!), give them souvenirs to take home. Fill silver or red bags with a toy spaceship, a map of the constellations, and a packet of Space Dust.

Live long and party!

Panto Party

**Who says pantomimes are just for Christmas? Now you can enjoy
them anytime with this theatrical theme!**

Invitations

Design a panto playbill for your party invitations, with the birthday child as the
star! Include a photo next to their name, and suggest a part for them to play –
Aladdin, Cinderella, Dick Whittington, etc.

Don't forget to include the name of the theatre (your address), and the date
and time of the performance.

Now, on with the show!

Decoration

You'll need plenty of card to decorate your party room. Tape several sheets of
card together, and paint a variety of pantomime scenes on to them.

You could design Widow Twankey's laundry, the Cave of Wonders, Snow
White's cottage, or any other panto setting.

Cut around the top and sides of your scenery, and attach them to the walls.

You can also place a variety of 'props' around the room, and hang curtains over the doorway to make the room look like the wing space of a theatre.

Why not make a 'Stage Door' sign to hang above the doorway as your panto cast arrives?

Costumes

Provide a pile of dressing up clothes for your guests (a trip to the local charity shop is in order), and encourage the kids to bring any old clothes of their own.

Set aside a separate dressing room, complete with craft materials such as glue, scissors and safety pins – and help your guests to create a costume to wear for the party as an opening activity. Search the Internet for some panto costume ideas.

Games

With the audience in their seats, and your cast ready in the wings – time to raise the curtain, and have some fun with these great games:

HE'S BEHIND YOU! A quick fire question game to try to identify your guests' friends!

One player sits in a chair, facing you, with all the other guests out of their line of vision. One of this player's friends is chosen to stand directly behind the chair. The player has to ask five questions that can be answered with 'yes' or 'no' to try to guess the identity of their friend.

They could ask you 'Is it a boy?', 'Is he tall?', 'Does he go to school with me?', etc. After five questions, they must try to guess who the friend is. If they are correct, they get to stay in the chair, and another friend is chosen to stand behind them. If they answer incorrectly, the person behind the chair takes their place, and must guess the identity of a friend of their own.

OH NO, IT ISN'T! A very silly, simple game!

One player is blindfolded, and sits at a table, facing the rest of the party guests. An object is placed in front of the blindfolded player, who must feel it, and work out what it is.

When they think they know, they must guess out loud. If they are incorrect, the other party guests shout out, 'Oh no, it isn't!' or in the case of a correct guess, 'Oh yes, it is!'

Each player has one minute to figure out what their object is, then another player is blindfolded, and another object offered.

I said it was silly!

SONG SHEET! Every pantomime has a song sheet where lyrics to a famous song are lowered down for the audience to sing along.

In this version, split the guests into two teams, and pin a sheet of card onto opposite walls as two blank song sheets.

Each team is given a selection of words on pieces of card, most of which will form a verse to a popular song when placed in the correct order. Include a few extra words as red herrings, and stick some double sided tape to the backs of the words.

When the game starts, the first player from each team must grab a word, and stick it to the song sheet. Then the next player gets to choose a word, and tries to put it into the correct order. The game keeps going as player after player adds a word, and tries to form the lyrics to the song.

To help the players along, play the song as background music to the game – and see if the teams can complete the verse before the music ends.

The first team to get all the words in the right order wins the game.

Food

After exerting themselves with your panto games, your guests will be ready for their interval snacks! Let's see what Sarah the Cook has to offer!

TWANKEY'S TWINKIES! While Twinkies are a favourite snack in the US, they haven't quite made the trip across the Atlantic to the UK. While this idea won't give you the genuine product, they're still very tasty!

Cut sponge fingers in half lengthways, and spread a combination of jam and butter cream in the middle before pressing the two halves back together. Sprinkle a little icing sugar over the top and serve to your guests.

Delicious!

GIVE-AWAYS! Don't forget the age old panto tradition of throwing packets of sweets and crisps into the audience! Wander around the room with a basket full of treats and toss them to each of your guests. Make sure that everybody gets one, and that – for the sake of your carpet – you only throw items that are securely sealed!

Party Bags

Send your panto cast hi-hoing their way home by filling a brightly coloured bag with a joke book, some sweets, and a practical joke or two!

A great party? Oh yes it is!

Party Political

**Order, order! Would the members please cast their votes
on how much they intend to enjoy this party theme!**

Invitations

Invite guests to party in the house with a specially designed campaign leaflet!
Include the venue for your 'conference', and the date and time of the rally you
want the party faithful to attend.

You could also add a picture of the birthday child as Prime Minister, and a few
of their policies, such as:

◆ To have fun for the entire party.
◆ To ban boredom in all its forms.
◆ To eat as much food as possible!

Decoration

Recreate the House of Commons in your living room by drawing ten rows of ten
empty seats on pieces of card and cutting them out.

The seats don't have to be life-sized, but they should be painted green (your kids can do this for you) and, when dry, pinned up on opposite sides of the room – five to each wall.

You'll also need to cut 50 circles from purple crepe paper, and 50 from orange. Simply keep the rolls of paper folded up, and draw around a drinking glass as many times as you can on one of the sides. When you cut the circles out, cut through the entire roll. The reason for these circles will be explained later.

Costumes

The costumes for this party are among the simplest to make – rosettes!

Cut a 6cm circle of card and three circles of crepe paper (8cm, 6cm and 4cm) for each guest. Place the card circle at the back, and then the crepe paper on top in size order, starting with the largest, and staple them in the centre. Now ruffle the edges of the crepe paper circles to make them stand up from the card.

Next, staple two 10cm 'ribbons' of crepe paper to the back of the rosette so that they dangle below it, and tape a safety pin to the back.

Make half of your rosettes purple and half orange – these will be your two political party colours for the games that follow.

Games

Split your party guests up according to their rosettes, and get them to sit on either side of the room. They'll be playing the games that follow in order to win MPs for their side of the house. Each game will be worth a certain number of new party members, which will be shown by sticking appropriately coloured circles onto the empty seats on the walls.

At the end of the party, the team with the highest number of MPs has won the election!

Now, let's get back to basics with some fun!

KISS THE BABY! Politicians are famous for kissing babies while they're out campaigning – and your party guests will be no different!

On a large sheet of paper (you could use the back of a length of wallpaper) draw three life-sized babies. Pin this paper at your guests' head height to a wall, and clear any obstacles from in front of it.

Now, cut three sets of large lips from card (approx. 6cm in length) and paint them red. Onto the back of the lips, tape a 'V' shaped piece of card so that it stands up like a handle. Place the lips face down on a table, next to a saucer filled with PVA glue.

To play the game, each player is blindfolded in turn, and has one minute to grab a set of lips between their teeth, dip it in the glue, and use it to kiss the babies on the wall. Then they must find their way back to the table to get the other sets of lips, and repeat the kisses.

After all three sets of lips have been used, the blindfold is removed, and the player sees how well they have done. Award them ten new MPs for a direct kiss on a baby's face, and five for anywhere else on the body.

Then, carefully remove the lips from the wall, blindfold the next player, and carry on kissing!

LOOPY LAWS. Did you know that, in the UK, sticking a postage stamp onto a letter upside down is an act of treason? Or that in Australia all taxis must carry a bale of hay?

These are just some of the ridiculous rulings that still exist around the world, and your political parties are about to guess whether they are true or not.

Make a list of 20 loopy laws – ten real, and ten made up. You can find some hilarious real laws at *www.dumblaws.com*

Each team should sit in front of their MPs' benches while you read out these laws one at a time. After each law the team must confer, and decide whether they think the law is real or not, and then hold up a card that says either true or false (you can make these before the game starts). If the team is correct, they win five new MPs – then it's on to the next law!

CAMPAIGN TRAIL! A fast and furious hunt for votes!

Make two ballot boxes by cutting a slot in the tops of two cardboard boxes and painting one orange, and the other purple. Now, cut up 100 slips of paper, and mark half with a purple cross and half with orange. Hide these votes all over the house before the party begins.

When the game starts, the guests have ten minutes to search the house and find as many votes that belong to their party as they can, and post them in the ballot boxes. However, players can only hold one vote at a time (they can't collect ten and post them all at once), and must not touch votes belonging to the opposing party.

After the time is up, the votes are counted, and the winning team is awarded 20 new MPs!

Food

Treat your guests to the finest cuisine that the House's restaurant can supply!

STRAWBERRIES AND CREAM. Make a large strawberry jelly but, before it sets completely, add some real strawberry pieces and a few splashes of cream and put it back into the fridge. To serve, separate the jelly into bowls, and pour extra cream on top!

NON-ALCOHOLIC CHAMPAGNE. Easy to make – just mix a bottle of sparkling water with a carton of apple juice, tell your guests it's champagne, and let their imaginations do the rest!

Party Bags

Treat your MPs to a bag in their party colours packed with a pad and pencils (for taking notes in Parliament), and some sweets to chew during the boring bits!

My vote is on a great party!

Passport Party

Around the world in 80 laughs with a party that spans the globe!

Invitations

In order to get into the party, your guests will each need a passport – and this will also double as their invitation!

The passports are quite simple to make. Cut two sheets of A4 paper in half, then fold them in half again to create the inner pages for the passport. To make the cover, cut a sheet of red A4 card in half, and fold it over. Slip the pages inside the cover, and staple the passport together.

Design an official looking emblem on a computer, then print them off and stick them to the covers of the passports to finish them off.

Inside the front page, write your guest's name, and leave a space for a photograph (your guests can stick one in themselves). Make a passport for each of your guests, and a few to keep as spares.

To complete the invitations, design and print off a 10cm by 20cm airline ticket for each guest on the computer. Simply add a picture of an aeroplane (your word processor's clip art collection should have one), make up an airline name (you could use the birthday child's surname), and invite your guests to take off on a trip around the world. Don't forget to include the time and date of the flight, where it departs from, and remind all passengers to bring their passports with them.

Now, you're almost ready for take off!

Decoration

Make your guests' arrival to the party as safe and secure as possible! Make an airline gate sign to hang over the front door – a piece of yellow card with 'Gate 28' in big, black letters!

Inside the hallway, all passengers will have to pass through a security check. Make a metal detector by sticking lengths of card around a doorframe, and pressing a button on a mobile 'phone to make a 'blip' sound as your guests pass through!

Your party room should be as exciting as possible! Cover the walls with maps and pictures of holiday destinations cut from holiday brochures (your local travel agent will be only too happy to give these away). Hang a few inflatable globes and model aeroplanes from the ceiling with cotton.

Finally, create the four corners of the world in the four corners of your living room! Choose four countries, and decorate the corners of your party room accordingly. This is a great pre-party activity for your own kids.

For Australia, you could stick cardboard boomerangs to the wall, make a didgeridoo by painting a long cardboard tube, and add a toy kangaroo. France could have an Eiffel Tower cut from card, French flags, and road signs showing distances to Paris, Cannes and Bordeaux.

What suggestions do your kids have for the two remaining countries?

Costumes

This party has the simplest costume theme ever – holidays in the sun!

Ask your guests to come dressed in shorts, t-shirts and flip-flops. They could wear sunglasses and hats, have cameras around their necks, and maybe even carry a beach ball or bucket and spade with them!

You could make Hawaiian shirts for the party by cutting shapes from brightly coloured crepe paper and sticking them to plain, old school shirts. Why not run this as an activity as your guests are arriving?

Games

Now that the trip has begun, it's time to entertain your passengers with these travel games!

Instead of awarding points, design and print off 'stamps' to stick into your guests' passports at the end of each game. You could make them look like the stamps they'd receive at passport control counters as they travel – with the date and name of the country they're entering. Your guests would be competing to see how many of these stamps they can collect by the end of their journey.

Time to play!

WHERE IN THE WORLD? A fast paced quiz game that will turn your guests map manic!

Split your guests into two teams, and sit them on the floor. In front of each team stick a map of the world, and hand out felt tip pens.

When the game starts, ask questions to which the answers are the names of countries or major cities. Instead of shouting out the answers to these questions, one player from each team must jump up and draw a cross on their map to show their guess.

For example, if you were to ask, 'Moscow is the capital city of which country?', the teams would have to mark a cross inside Russia to be correct.

The teams have 30 seconds after each question in which to confer, and then mark the map. Each team member should take it in turn to be the one to answer with their pen.

Here are a few sample questions; you could choose others from a quiz book, or simply make them up yourself:

- In which city does the President of the USA live? (Washington)
- Which country used to be separated into east and west by the Berlin Wall? (Germany)
- With South Korea, which other country hosted the 2002 World Cup? (Japan)

At the end of the game, the team with the most correct answers wins a stamp inside their passports from one of the countries used in the quiz!

LOST AND FOUND. Players sit in a circle in the centre of the room, and prepare for chaos!

Shout out the name of a country. Everyone must jump up and grab an item that is related to it. For Canada they could choose a picture of a Mountie or a maple leaf; for China they could snatch up some chopsticks, or a piece of card with Chinese writing on.

The first three players to sit back down with an item from that country each win a stamp in their passport. Then it's time to call out another country, and play again!

Make sure you have plenty of items to grab for each country, and that they are spaced around the room so that everyone has a chance to win.

POSTCARDS FROM THE EDGE. A slightly more sedate game after the two previous bouts of madness!

Number blank postcards in the top left-hand corner from '1' upwards, then give one to each guest. Provide plenty of coloured pens and pencils, and lots of table or floor space for them to use.

Your guests now have ten minutes to design a postcard for a famous place, and colour it in. They could draw a red double decker bus to signify London, or a picture of Mickey Mouse to show Disneyland.

When they have finished, stick all the postcards up on a wall, and give each player a sheet of paper with numbers down the side that match the number of cards. The guests then have another ten minutes to study the cards, and write down their guesses as to where they think each card represents. Remind them to write their names at the top of their sheet of paper.

When the time is up, they should hand their sheets in to you, and you can mark them while they are eating. Award passport stickers to the players with the most correct guesses, and also to those with the best designed cards.

Food

The great thing about world travel is the opportunity to sample food from many different countries. Try these international ideas for your food table:

PIZZA. A favourite from Italy that all kids will love – but how do you solve the eternal problem of toppings they might not like? Simple, just cook plain cheese pizzas, cut them into slices, and provide bowls of toppings for your guests to sprinkle on themselves! Use tomatoes, sweet corn, pepperoni, pineapple, onion, etc. They'll create some strange, but succulent, combinations!

TACOS. A marvellous meal from magical Mexico! You should be able to find taco kits in your local supermarket. You just warm the taco shells in the microwave, add spiced mince beef, cheese and salad for a tasty taco treat!

Party Bags

Use a home-made stencil to mark an aeroplane on the side of plain carrier bags to make it look as though your guests have just come through airport customs as their parents pick them up.

Fill these bags with worldly wonders such as postcards, maps, and model aeroplane kits and they'll be sure to travel with you again next year!

Now you can relax before the jet-lag kicks in!

Pooh Party

Play in the 100 Aker Wood with Winnie The Pooh,
Piglet and Tigger, too! Perfect for younger kids.

Invitations

Draw and cut out a picture of Pooh Bear for each invitation – you could get your birthday child to help colour them in.

Make Pooh's t-shirt from red crepe paper, but just attach it at the top. Underneath, write your invitation on his tummy, giving the date and time of the party. You could even copy one of Pooh's famous Hums for your guests to sing on the way:

Tra-la-la, tra-la-la,
Tra-la-la, tra-la-la,
Rum-tum-tiddle-um-tum.
Tiddle-iddle, tiddle-iddle,
Tiddle-iddle, tiddle-iddle,
Rum-tum-tum-tiddle-um.

Warn your guests to watch out for Heffalumps and Woozles on the way! They should be safe, however, as Pooh Bear made a very handy Hole For Heffalumps to catch them.

Decoration

There's only one way to decorate your party room – disguise it as the 100 Aker Wood where Christopher Robin played with his friends.

Cover the walls with trees made from brown and green crepe paper. Your birthday child could help you with the decorating by sticking leaves onto the branches. Make logs to place around the room by rolling a sheet of card around a cardboard box, and painting it brown. When it's dry, use a black marker pen to draw a wood effect onto the paint.

Mark all the special places in the wood with card signposts: Rabbit's house, the sandy pit where Roo plays, Eeyore's gloomy place, and the tree where the Wozzle Wasn't! Stick the signs to the walls around the room so that your guests don't get lost when they arrive!

One thing is still missing – Pooh's Hunny Pot! Cover a small bucket with red crepe paper, and screw up lots of yellow paper to push inside. Add a few yellow dribbles around the rim, and paint HUNNY on the front in childish writing.

There's a great map of the 100 Aker Wood for you to work from at: *www.lavasurfer.com/pooh-100newmap.html*

Costumes

In your invitations, ask your guests to come to the party dressed as their favourite character from the Winnie The Pooh stories.

They could wear a brown jump-suit, and have a long tail made from a stuffed stocking to be Roo. Cover a black t-shirt and pair of trousers in orange crepe paper stripes for Tigger (use the other stocking for his tail). For Pooh himself, colour their skin with orange face paint, and wear a red t-shirt.

The easiest of all the costumes is Christopher Robin. Have a few pairs of shorts and t-shirts handy in case anyone arrives without a costume and feels left out.

Games

Even though he's a bear of very little brain, Pooh loves to play with his friends. Maybe they've tried some of these games:

WHERE'S EEYORE'S TAIL? Eeyore is miserable - he's lost his tail again. Can the kids help to find it for him?

Make the tail by doubling over a length of grey material, and stitching it up the side. Sew a black tassle to the end and you have Eeyore's frequently lost appendage.

Get your guests to close their eyes tight, then hide the tail somewhere in the wood - inside a log, behind a tree, or even in Pooh's Hunny Pot!

Your guests must open their eyes, and try to be the first to find it! If they're having trouble, tell them when they're getting warmer or colder.

When Eeyore's tail is finally discovered, everyone closes their eyes again, and the tail is lost once more.

Poor Eeyore!

BOUNCY, TROUNCY, FLOUNCY, POUNCY! The most excitable inhabitant of the wood comes to play in this game filled with bounce power!

Ask the kids what Tigger is famous for, and they'll all shout back 'Bouncing!' That's because his top is made out of rubber, and his bottom is made out of springs.

Play some music (if you have 'The Wonderful Thing About Tiggers!' then use that), and get your guests to bounce along to the music. Stop the song, and everyone has to stand as still as they can until the music starts again.

There are no winners or losers in this game, just lots of bouncing and fun, fun, fun, fun, fun!

Remember to play this game before your guests have eaten!

POOH STICKS. It might be difficult to play Pooh's favourite game without a river, but here's a version you can play inside with just two drinking straws.

Choose two players, and ask them to kneel down. Place a straw side-on in front of them and, when you shout go, they must blow their straw and be the first to reach the winning post (pace one of your logs a few metres away).

Remind everyone that they must only blow their straw, and not touch it with their hands.

When the game is over, choose two new players, and have another game of Pooh Sticks!

Food

Pooh's got a Rumbly in his Tumbly. It's time for tea!

HUNNY. Although it's unlikely that your young guests will actually like real honey, you can spread caramel sauce over vanilla ice cream and pretend it is Pooh's favourite food. For added effect, why not pour the sauce from a pot with HUNNY written along the side?

CHRISTOPHER ROBIN'S CAKE. Most of the other animals in the 100 Aker Wood like foods that taste fairly horrible. Piglet like Haycorns, Eeyore eats thistles, and Tigger will touch nothing except extract of malt!

Only Christopher Robin has an edible favourite - cake, and lots of it. Buy some small Winnie The Pooh characters to sit on top of your birthday child's cake, making sure there are enough for everyone to take one of the toys home.

Perhaps you could even bake a cake in the shape of Pooh Bear himself?

Party Bags

When Kanga calls, it's time for Pooh and his friends to head home for the night.

Make bags covered with Pooh pictures to give out as they leave containing Winnie The Pooh books, sweets, and of course a red balloon so that Pooh can float up to get to the honey in the bee hive.

As the great bear himself once said, 'Nobody can be uncheered with a balloon!'

Pyramids

**Enter the Pharaoh's tomb in search of hidden treasure, but one
wrong move and you might wake Mummy!**

Invitations

Make an ancient Egyptian scroll to invite your guests to this party!

Wipe a wet teabag over a sheet of white paper to give it an old, faded look.
Then, when it's dry, draw a border of hieroglyphic characters. You can see what
they look like at *www.greatscott.com/hiero/*

In the middle of your scroll, write of treasure buried deep within a tomb, which
is protected by a Mummy's curse. Explain that you're gathering together a team
of explorers to search for the treasure, and that anyone brave enough should
meet at the address of the party at a particular time, on a particular day. Close
by wishing everyone good luck, then roll the scroll up, and tie it with a ribbon.

Make one of these for each guest, and hand them out.

Decoration

Transform your party room into the hidden tomb, deep within the pyramid with a
few simple craft materials, and lots of gold paint!

Cover sheets of card with hieroglyphic writing and strange symbols, and pin them to the walls. Paint cardboard boxes in bright colours, and fill them with stones, wrapped in coloured foil to look like chests of gems.

Paint plastic cups, wooden spoons and old books gold, and lay them on every available surface. The more golden items you have, the richer your Pharaoh will be!

Roll up sheets of card, and make red and yellow crepe paper flames to stick out of the top. Pin these torches around the walls at regular intervals.

Finally, glue four or five cardboard boxes on top of one another. Tape their top flaps together to form a door, and paint a colourful picture of the Pharaoh on the front. Stand this sarcophagus against the wall; could the Mummy be hiding inside?

Costumes

Your party guests must be well equipped if they are to venture inside the pyramid, and down into the tomb. In your invites, ask them to come to the party wearing shorts, shirts and hats.

As they arrive, your guests can make themselves pieces of explorers' equipment to take with them. They can create a pair of binoculars by glueing together two toilet roll tubes, painting them black, and hanging them around their necks with string. They'll need maps, which they can draw on more pieces of tea bag soaked parchment.

Now, it's time to venture into the dark...

Games

With the treasures of the tomb around them, your brave team of explorers can enjoy themselves with a few pyramid pastimes!

CURSE OF THE PHARAOH! Oh no! By opening the tomb, your guests have brought a dreadful curse upon themselves! But, who is responsible? Play this game and find out.

One explorer is chosen to step inside the Mummy's sarcophagus. They must close their eyes tight, and promise not to peep out.

When the explorer is inside, another player is chosen to have the Pharaoh's curse. All of the guests – apart from the person hidden away – should know who this is.

Bring the explorer back out, and start the game. Everyone must wander around the tomb, examining the objects they find around them. After a little while, the player chosen to carry the curse uses it, and sticks their tongue out at another guest. That guest must scream, and drop to the floor!

Everyone stops, and the explorer must try to guess who it is that passed on the curse. If they are right, the game is over, and another explorer is chosen. If they are not right, the cursed player sits out, and the game continues.

One by one, as the players are cursed and drop out, the explorer comes closer to spotting the guest with the curse. But will they be caught before everyone is bumped off?

I WANT MY MUMMY! Fast, frantic and funny!
Split your guests into groups of three, and give each team three toilet rolls. One of each trio is chosen to be the Mummy.

When the game starts, the players have three minutes to transform their respective Mummies by covering them from head to toe in toilet roll bandages! The Mummies mustn't help, they have to stand still while they are wrapped up!

At the end of the game, inspect the Mummies to see which is the best dressed – then they can all burst out of their bandages with a terrifying roar!

WALK LIKE AN EGYPTIAN. Was this really how the pyramids were built?
For this game, you'll need an empty cardboard box for each player. Tape the boxes closed, and paint them to look like blocks of stone.

Play some Egyptian sounding music – perhaps The Sand Dance, or Walk Like An Egyptian by The Bangles. While the music plays, the guests must stagger around the room, carrying their blocks, making them look as heavy as possible.

After a while, stop the song and shout out a number from two to ten. The players must then rush together and build a pile of that number of blocks.

Some of the numbers will mean that everyone gets to use their block, and others won't – but you'll be guaranteed a lot of scrabbling about and giggles!

When the towers have been built, start the music again. Time for everyone to retrieve their stone, and carry them around the room again.

End the game with the same number as you have guests and watch them try to build a huge tower!

Food

After a hard day's exploring, your heroes will need to eat. Try these Mummified munchies on them:

FRUIT OF THE NILE. Sounds simple, just lots and lots of fresh fruit. It's what kept the Kings strong and the slaves even stronger.

However, even the food has been cursed! Explorers can choke if they eat their own fruit. The answer is simple, they have to feed each other! Watch as your guests wrap their arms around each other to gobble grapes and attack apples. Making food fun!

ASSES' MILK. Cleopatra is famed for bathing in it – but don't tell your guests or they won't touch the stuff!

Serve ice cold milk in golden goblets and, for a bit of excitement, add a drop of food colouring to each glass and watch the milk change colour before their eyes!

Party Bags

When all the riches have been collected, it's time for the explorers to head off in search of deeper tombs!

Provide them each with a simple cloth bag (fold a piece of material in half and stitch up the sides), into which they can drop their horde. They're allowed to take anything that will fit in their bags – jewels, sweets, fruit – even the golden plates.

It'll save you clearing up when they've gone home!

Rainbow

A bright, colourful party theme ideal for younger kids!

Invitations

Get your kids to help you create the invitations to this party.

Use a paper plate for each guest, and let your kids paint a rainbow around the edge, letting each colour dry before they add the next, so that the paint doesn't run.

When they're all dry, write your party invitation in the centre, asking each of your guests to wear bright, primary colours for the day!

Now, punch a hole in the centre of the plate, and use a paper fastener to loosely attach it to a strip of sturdy card. You should now be able to spin the plate, making amazing rainbow effects as the colours whiz around!

Decoration

This is a simple party to decorate – just lots of bright, solid colours!

Buy a roll or two of cheap wallpaper from a DIY shop, and pin it up to one wall, with the plain back showing. As your guests arrive, give them rolls of coloured paper and safety scissors. They can cut out shapes and patterns to stick to this wall with paper glue sticks, creating a colourful mural for the party. Make sure they know only to stick things onto the special sections of wallpaper!

Pin lengths of crepe paper to the ceiling to create a rainbow. Let one end of each sheet dangle free so that the rainbow moves in the breeze!

Cover tables with crepe paper, and use bright napkins and plastic cutlery to make it all look crazy and colourful!

Costumes

The only real costume theme is colour. Your guests should arrive in bright reds, blues, greens and yellows – adding to the colourful design of your party room.

Why not use face paint to draw designs on your guests' cheeks as they arrive? Ask each guest to choose a colour and a shape for each cheek.

Games

Time for some rainbow based fun as your guests take part in games using all the colours around them!

RAINBOW RUN. Cut squares of red, blue, yellow and green, and pin one to each of the four corners of the room. Next, make identical smaller cards, and drop them into a cardboard box covered with bright wrapping paper.

When the game starts, play a CD, and your guests dance in the middle of the room. After a while, stop the music, and the players must choose one of the four colours, and run to that corner.

When everyone has chosen, reach into the box, and pull out one of the cards. Whoever is standing in the corresponding corner wins that round! Get them to cheer whenever they are the winners. Then, bring everyone back into the centre of the room, play the music, and start dancing again!

Nobody is 'out' or wins prizes in this game, it's just a bit of colourful fun to get everyone moving around.

BLOW ART. A fun paint activity for your guests to enjoy!

Cover a table with plastic bin liners to protect the surface, and lay plenty of newspaper on top. Give each of your guests an apron or old shirt to wear.

Provide plenty of bright poster paint, sheets of paper and straws. The kids must drop blobs of paint onto their paper (make sure it is nice and watery), then use the straws to blow the colours into unusual shapes and patterns. Make sure you explain that they must only blow through the straws, and never suck!

Blow different colours of paint across each other to see how they mix together.

Leave the pictures to dry, then pin them onto the colour wall for the rest of the party!

MIX & MATCH. Test your party guests' knowledge of the world around them with this game of colours and shapes.

Make two sets of cards - one with colours on, and the other with objects. Don't worry if you use the same colour more than once.

To play the game, sit the kids in the centre of the room, and pick a card from each pile. Perhaps you might choose 'green' and 'vegetable'. Read the cards out, and your guests must put their hands in the air if they can think of something that matches both cards. So, for green vegetable, they might say 'cucumber', 'lettuce' or 'cabbage'.

When you have had a few correct answers, pick two new cards, and try again. What will the kids come up with for red vehicle, white animal, or even yellow food?

Food

Speaking of food - even the meal at your Rainbow Party can be as colourful as you want to make it! Why not try these bright bites?

CRUNCHY COLOURS. Fill bowls with snacks of different colours for your guests to nibble at. Try orange carrots, green celery, red apples and yellow bananas.

RAINBOW CUBES! What looks like clear lemonade can be magically transformed to a myriad of different colours by adding special ice cubes!

Fill ice cube trays with water but, before you put them in the freezer, add a tint drop of food colouring to each cube. When they have set, your guests can drop one of these cubes into a glass of lemonade and watch their drink slowly change colour as the ice melts!

Party Bags

When it's time for home, hand out multi-coloured gift bags filled with small paint sets, pencils and sketch pads. Your guests can draw and colour pictures of the party when they get home. Don't forget to give them their blow-art pictures to pin up on their bedroom walls!

What a bright idea!

Rock 'n' Roll

**Flip, Flop & Fly back to the 50s to Shake, Rattle & Roll
with this rockin' party theme!**

Invitations

Everyone who is invited to this party gets a single invitation. By that, I mean your invites are actual singles!

Head down to your local charity shop or car boot sale, and pick up enough 45rpm singles so that you have one for each party guest, and a few spare. It doesn't matter which artists they are (most of your guests won't know how to play them on their CD players, anyway!)

When you get them home, make new sleeves for them out of plain card, and design a picture for the front on a PC. You could scan in a picture of the birthday child holding a guitar, or singing into a microphone, and add a catchy title such as Come To My Rockin' Party!.

Next, print off circular labels to stick onto the centre of the singles. These will cover the original record labels, and will be where you give details of the party; where and when it will take place. You'll need two of these for each single.

Finally, on the back of the record sleeve, ask the boys to come wearing jeans and a shirt, and the girls to wear long skirts and t-shirts.

Then hand out your record invitations!

Decoration

Turn your party room into a 1950's diner.

Cut a life-sized cardboard jukebox to stick to one wall, and paint it in bright colours. Fill the remaining walls with posters of famous rock 'n' roll stars such as Elvis Presley, Buddy Holly and Chuck Berry.

Place tables and chairs at regular intervals around the walls, leaving the centre of the room free for games and dancing. You could photocopy pieces of sheet music and tape them together to make disposable tablecloths.

Finally, play a rock 'n' roll CD in the background as your guests arrive.

Costumes

Hopefully your guests will have followed the instructions on the backs of their invitations, and come dressed appropriately – but there are still a few extras you can add as a fun warm-up activity.

For the girls, put their hair in ponytails and give them a few books to carry as though they were on their way home from high school. Quiff the boys' hair with gel, and get them to make bootlace ties from a bootlace, and a piece of tin foil to act as a clasp.

Games

Think your rockers and rollers are too cool to play some party games? That'll be the day...

ROCK AROUND THE CLOCK. To get things going, play this musical game that will have them dancing through time.

On the walls around the room, stick up cards with the numbers 1 to 12 in clockwise order – so the numbers 12 and 6 are opposite each other, as are 3 and 9, etc.

Gather your guests into the centre of the room, and play a rock 'n' roll CD for them to dance to. After a short while, stop the music, and call out a time, such as 'one o'clock!', 'six o'clock!', etc.

The players then have to gather together at that time on the clock as quickly as they can. Take care that any younger guests aren't knocked over in the dash to reach the right number.

As the game progresses, add some more difficult times to the game. For 'half past seven' the players would need to stand between the numbers seven and eight. Or split them into boys and girls – one group for the hour hand, and the other for the minute hand of the clock. At 'twenty to three' the boys would have to run to the number eight while the girls gathered between two and three.

Keep playing until everyone is worn out from dancing!

MAKING MUSIC. Draw a musical stave (five horizontal lines) onto two large pieces of card, and stick them side by side on one wall. Next, cut five notes from black card for each stave. If you know anything about music (or can borrow a book from the library), make them a variety of notes.

Finally, draw a third stave onto a smaller piece of card, and draw the five notes onto it at various places. Stick this in between the two larger staves, and you're ready to play.

Split the group into two teams, and sit each team opposite one of the two large staves. Place the five notes for each team on a table next to them, and stick some double sided tape onto the back of them. Each team must then choose one player to be their 'composer'. Just as Beethoven was deaf – these composers will be blind! Blindfold these two players with lengths of material, and stand them next to the tables where their notes are.

When the game starts, the teams will have three minutes to match the complete stave in the middle by shouting directions to their blind composer. They can call out which note to pick up, which direction to walk in, and where to stick it to the chart. The other team members must remain where they are, and can't touch their composer, or their notes.

When both teams have finished placing their notes, or the time is up, remove the composers' blindfolds to show them how they have done. Award ten points to a team for each note in the correct place, and a bonus ten points if all the notes are in the right order.

To play again, stick a new order of notes in the centre of the wall, blindfold two new composers, and make music one more time!

RAVE ON! Your guests become the rock 'n' roll stars!

Play a famous song from the 50s, and ask your guests to listen carefully, and try to work out which instruments are playing. There could be a guitar, bass, drums, piano, and a singer.

Split the guests up into groups of four or five, and provide them with a variety of craft materials: card, paper, toilet roll tubes, string, boxes, elastic bands, etc. Just about anything you can find. It's a good idea to fill a separate bin liner with materials for each of the groups (start collecting as far as you can before the party).

The groups then have ten minutes to make instruments from the materials in front of them. They could cut guitars from card, or stretch elastic bands over a plastic tub. Boxes and pencils make good drums, while a ball of newspaper taped to the top of a toilet roll tube can act as a microphone. Have scissors, tape and pens available for the groups to use.

When everyone has made their instruments, play the song again and let them rehearse miming along in the corners of the room. Remind them that it is only a bit of fun, and that they don't have to be note perfect!

Finally, ask each group to think of a name for themselves (the sillier the better), and come into the centre of the room in turn to perform to the song for the other groups, who can clap along, and cheer at the end.

Rock 'n' roll!

food

American diner food is, coincidentally, just the sort of stuff that kids love! Who's going to say no to these delicious delights?

BEEFBURGERS AND FRIES! The classic burger has been around long before fast food restaurants got their hands on them. Grill your burgers, and use low fat oven chips for a healthier version of the meal.

ICE CREAM SUNDAES. Pile layers of flavoured ice cream into tall glasses and suddenly, your guests will go very quiet as they all dive in!

Party Bags

Cover gift bags with lace for the girls, and a bootlace tie for the boys. Drop in a comb (essential for keeping those quiffs in order), and an autograph book and pen for collecting star studded signatures.
That party rocks!

Science Lab

Bunsen burners at the ready for an experimental party where only the craziest scientists are invited!

Invitations

Remember back to school when you were sitting in your physics class, writing up the results of yet another experiment? That's exactly how you're going to invite your kids' friends to this party! Listing equipment, method and results – like this:

Party Experiment by Tommy Donbavand
EQUIPMENT
One house at 28 Writer's Lane

Three hours, from 1pm to 4pm

Fifteen guests, including *Robert Parker*

Everyone will bring: one large white shirt

one pair of old, unwanted sunglasses

METHOD
On 9th July, I will gather my friends together to have a party based on science.
We'll play games, eat food and conduct weird and wonderful experiments.

RESULTS

Everyone will have a great time!

Change the details to fit your own, including the name of the guest for each invite, and fill the page up with diagrams of your party guests playing games and enjoying themselves.

Deliver your invites in envelopes marked TOP SECRET EXPERIMENT!

Decoration

To decorate your party room, you'll need lots of clear plastic items such as mineral water bottles, cups, cutlery, etc. Plus, visit your local DIY store to get a few lengths of plastic tubing.

Set up a table along one wall of your party room (a decorator's pasting table would be ideal), and start to assemble your plastic bits and pieces into something that looks like a mad scientist's laboratory.

Fill bottles with water, and add a few drops of food colouring (screw the lids on tight – it will stain your carpet if it spills). Run the plastic tubing from bottle to bottle, into cups, through clear plastic boxes, and into inflated sandwich bags. Lay plastic cutlery around the table to look like lab tools. Keep going until you have built what looks like a huge, complicated experiment!

Now cover the walls of the room with diagrams sketched onto card, pages from old science text books, and a blackboard filled with complex equations.

Costumes

In your invites, you asked your guests to bring a large white shirt (one of Dad's would be ideal). Pick up a few spares at a charity shop just in case.

Your guests should wear their shirts over their clothing like lab coats. If the shorts have a top pocket, fill it with pens and pencils.

Next, carefully press the lenses out of old pairs of sunglasses to make geeky looking specs!

To complete the effect, back-comb your guests' hair until it has a wild, crazy look. They could even practise a mad scientist style laugh while you're doing it!

Games

Time for the lab technicians to get down to business with these chemistry capers!

UP AND ATOM! Not only is this great fun to play, it also wins the award for my favourite title for a game in the book!

Stitch stripes of velcro along the tops of two baseball caps. Use one side of the velcro on one hat, and the opposite half on the other.

Next, get 20 or 30 table tennis balls, and stick patches of velcro onto those at regular intervals (if you can't get ping pong balls, screw up sheets of newspaper as tightly as you can, and tape them in place). Again, use one side of the velcro on half of the balls, and the opposite side on the other.

Split the group into two teams, and get them to choose one of their players to be the nucleus of an atom. These two players step into the centre of the room, put their hands in their pockets, and each wear one of the velcro covered caps.

Divide the balls evenly between the two teams – these will be the protons.

To play the game, the two teams must throw the balls into the air above the two baseball capped nuclei. They must duck under the shower of protons, and try to get as many of them to stick to the velcro on their heads as possible. Only half of the balls will stick to each cap.

If a ball misses and falls to the floor, the nucleus can kick it back to his or her team mates – but they mustn't take their hands out of their pockets, or touch the balls with any other part of their body.

When the time is up (two minutes is a good length for this experiment), the team with the highest number of protons stuck to their cap are the winners. Choose two more nuclei, swap the caps over, and play again.

LET'S GET FIZZICAL! This game is best played outdoors!

Again, split your guests into two teams, and stand each group at one end of the garden. Give each team a jug of vinegar and an egg cup.

Opposite each team, place an experiment – a jug with three tablespoons of baking soda and a few drops of food colouring inside (cover these jugs with pieces of card), and an empty glass.

When the game starts, the first player from each team must dip the egg cup into the vinegar, run down the garden, and empty it into the glass. Then they have to run back, hand the egg cup over to the next player, who fills it with vinegar, and runs to add it to their glass.

Keep this relay race going for three minutes (or longer if you have more players – everyone should get at least three runs with the egg cup).

When the time is up gather the teams around their experiments. Remove the pieces of card and place them underneath the jugs then, at the same time, pour the vinegar each team has transferred over the baking soda.

The two elements will react and start to fizz. Whichever team's mixtures fizzes the most is the winner.

IT'S ALIVE! A game of monster proportions!

Prepare several body parts for each team: a head (a cardboard box painted green); a body (a jumper stuffed with newspaper); legs (trousers filled the same way); two feet (stuffed socks); hands (gloves); and two metal bolts (cover two pencils with tin foil).

Ask each team a science question in turn. If they are correct, they are awarded with a body part for their monster, which they lie on the floor. When one team has won all the necessary parts, they must play for the two silver bolts. Only when they are pushed into the sides of their monster's head will the creature come alive, and they will have won the game!

Use questions from a science quiz book, such as:

◆ What is H2O? (Water)
◆ Which is stronger, gold or diamond? (Diamond)
◆ At what temperature does water boil? (100 degrees Celsius)

When one of the monsters has been created, the other team can grab the parts to finish theirs. After all, there's nothing lonelier than a single monster at a party – he'd have no body to go with! (Oh, never mind!)

Food

I'm certain that, if you were to examine the experiments in any modern science lab, you would find that the technicians were actually making their lunch, rather than studying physics or chemistry!

Maybe this would be their scientific selection:

BRAIN FOOD. Everyone knows that scientists need to be brainy, and that fish is the ultimate brain food!

So, serve fish fingers for their boffin power, and chips for... well, they just taste nice!

BIOLOGY BANQUET. Have you ever noticed how certain foods look like parts of the body? Give these a go...

Fried tomatoes (hearts), sausages (intestines), and hard boiled eggs (eyeballs!). Only kids could eat something so gruesome!

Party Bags

When the last experiment has been conducted, it's time for the mad scientists to go home and dream of tomorrow's explorations!

Help them on their way with clear bags packed with a magnifying glass, a pencil for jotting down results, and a sheet of experiments they can try at home (there are plenty to be found online, and in my book, *Boredom Busters*!).

Now, that's clever!

Skoolz owt!

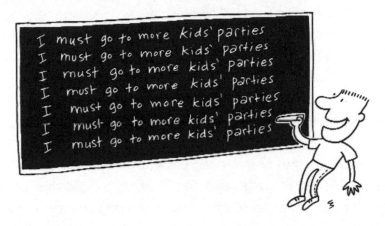

**Hey kids – leave those teachers alone! Had enough of school?
Fight back with this crazy classroom chaos!**

Invitations

Invitations to this party should be in the form of spoof school reports! Design a logo for the top of the letter, and split the page into four or five subjects, such as Maths, English and History.

Fill in these sections with made-up teachers' comments: 'History – Sam would have done better if she'd known today's date, let alone important ones in the past!' Individualise these comments for each of your guests.

At the bottom of the report, tell your guests that they are to 'See Me!', and add the date, time and location of the party. Post the reports out in brown, official looking envelopes!

Decoration

Decorate your party room by covering the walls in graffiti! Don't write this directly onto the walls, of course, instead, paint it onto sheets of card or paper and pin them up.

You could use incorrectly added up sums (2+2=7), badly spelled words (I Musst Spel Werds Bettter!), or even graffiti comments about the teachers from your child's school (Mr Lawrence has got a big bum!). Make sure that none of these teachers' kids are on the guest list, however!

To complete the classroom effect, make a blackboard by painting a sheet of wood with blackboard paint. Attach it to a wall, and provide chalks so that your guests can add their own comments during the party.

Costumes

In your invites, ask guests to attend the party in an old shirt (definitely NOT one of their school shirts!). Pick up a few extra shirts at your local charity shop just in case.

When the guests have arrived, give them some crepe paper, glue and scissors, and ask them to make a school tie. They can cut out basic tie shapes, and decorate them with spots, stripes, or any other patterns they can think of. Attach these home-made ties to their shirt collars with safety pins (don't tie them on with string, as this could hurt your guests!).

Games

Time for some school style silliness! Split your guests into two teams, and stick a score card for each onto the wall. Cut stars from gold card (or buy stickers) for the teams to win in each of the games.

TECHNO-TEACHER! This is more of an activity than a game, but your guests will really enjoy it.

Prior to your party, collect as many craft materials and useful bits and pieces as you can: empty cereal boxes, toilet roll tubes, yoghurt pots, etc. Fill two bin liners worth, and give one to each of the teams. Also provide them with glue, scissors, tape and string.

When the game starts, each team tips out the contents of their craft bag, and has half an hour to build a robot teacher from what is inside.

They can paint on x-ray eyes so that their teacher can spot who hasn't done their homework; an extendible arm to confiscate pupils' toys without ever leaving their desk; or even fingertips that are made of chalk to enable them to write on the board faster than ever. The only limit is their imagination!

LET THAT BE A LESSON! A fast-paced game that will leave your guests out of breath!

To play this game, the players find an empty space, and face you. You then call out a series of school lessons, and the players must quickly act out a movement connected to it:

HISTORY – Act out a sword battle.
BIOLOGY – Pretend to pull organs from stomach!
MATHS – Add up complicated sums on fingers.
ENGLISH – Sit down and scribble away writing a book.
CHEMISTRY – Mix chemicals together, big explosion.
GEOGRAPHY – Dig in the ground on a field trip.

Call out the lessons, getting faster as the game progresses, making sure that the players manage to keep up.

It's classroom chaos!

SOUPER DOUPER! Things are about to get messy, so spread plenty of towels and newspaper on the floor before you start this game!

You'll need two large washing up bowls. Fill each bowl three quarters of the way with water, and add a dash of milk and a handful of porridge oats to cloud the mixture.

Now, drop a variety of edible bits and pieces into each bowl; boiled sweets, slices of apple, grapes, sprouts – anything you can find. Now the fun starts.

Place each of the bowls filled with the sloppy soup mix at one end of the room, and line the two teams up at the other end. Put a large plate next to each of the bowls.

When the game starts, the first player in each team must run up to their washing up bowl, kneel in front of it with their hands behind their back, and dip their face into the soup to try to find an edible bit. When they have grabbed one with their teeth, they drop it onto the plate, and run back to their team – when the next player takes over.

The game continues until all players on one of the teams have dunked into the soup three times. Then, the bits of food on the plate are added up, and the team with the highest number are awarded ten gold stars!

Please remind all players to hold their breath while grabbing bits of food with their mouths, and watch that no-one gets anything stuck in their throats. Always supervise this game with two or more adults.

Food

After dipping their faces in school soup, your guests may not be that hungry – but here's a way to tempt them with tasty treats!

SANDWICH SURPRISE! Provide the bread and a whole host of ingredients for your guests to invent their own school sandwiches! What will banana, jam and crisps taste like? Or how about chocolate and jelly beans? Award gold stars for the most ridiculous ideas!

CHEESY CHIPS! All kids love chips, but have you tried them this way? Make a plate of low fat oven chips, and smother them in melted cheese sauce. It's tastier than it sounds!

Party Bags

As the bell rings for home time, fill some school lunch bags with pens, pencils, comics, and perhaps a practical joke or two to liven up the next school day. Hand them out, and prepare to deny all knowledge!
Full marks for a fun party!

Superheroes

**Is it a bird? Is it a plane? No, it's a superhero party,
so wear your underpants on the outside, and fly by!**

Invitations

Superheroes need to maintain their secret identities, so you can't invite them openly to the party, or everyone will know who they really are!

To avoid this, print off party invitations on white paper, leaving off the guest's name, the date, time and place – like this:

Come to a Party!
TO:
AT:
DATE:
TIME:

Then, with a white crayon, or sharpened wax candle, fill in the blank details. When you hand out your invites, explain that your guests will need to use their x-ray vision to read their invitation – or they could lightly shade over the wax with a pencil, whichever is easier!

To make the invites even more secret, seal them in brown envelopes, write 'TOP SECRET' on the front in red pen, and pass them secretly to your potential guests.

Decoration

A superhero party would take place out of view of any snooping reporters or sinister bad guys – so the ideal place to have it is in a secret hideout, like the Batcave!

To transform your room into a hideout, collect as many cardboard boxes as you can, and paint them silver. Draw on dials, lights, and computer readouts – and stick on bottle tops as buttons and switches.

Create weird looking equipment from any odds and ends you can find. What could you do with the inside of a broken video recorder, some rubber tubing and an empty cereal box?

Finally, fill some folders with sheets of paper, and stick photos of imaginary bad guys on the front. You could use pictures of family members, or your kids' teachers, and give them names such as The Smell, or Idioso!

Leave these folders lying around to look like cases your superheroes are still working on.

Costumes

This is a great opportunity for a built in activity to start the party with a swing. Head down to your local charity shop, and buy a bag full of old clothing, scraps of material, and any other odds and ends that might come in handy for costume making. Also provide enough pens, paper, scissors, glue and safety pins to go around.

When your guests have all arrived, start inventing superheroes! Help cut out cloaks, design logos, and make helmets - taking care to supervise the use of anything sharp. If your guests are likely to be shy, sketch a few ideas on paper and let them pick one out to make.

Each guest should give their superhero a name, and a special power, such as the ability to fly, bend iron bars, or eat school dinners without feeling ill!

Games

To avoid games where contestants are out, explain that your superheroes are playing for points which, at the end of the party, will be the number of times they have saved the city.

Why not design some spoof newspaper front pages leaving space in the headline for a superhero's name and picture underneath? During the party, take a picture of each superhero in action with a digital camera, and have another adult load them onto the computer, fill in the heroes' names and add the photographs. These would be great gifts to give your guests as they are leaving.

Now on to the fun!

BURST THE BAD GUYS! For this game, you'll need an old duvet cover and lots of balloons!

Blow up six balloons for each guest and, on five of each, draw a mean face with a marker pen. These are the bad guys! On the final balloon, draw a smiling face – the innocent bystander!

To play the game, put the first six balloons inside the duvet cover, shake them up, and drop the cover onto the floor. The first player must crawl onto the cover, and has one minute to find and burst five of the balloons by squeezing them in their hands, or stamping on them.

After the balloons have popped, remove the remaining balloon. If it is the innocent bystander, the superhero wins 10 points!

Stuff the next six balloons into the cover, and let the next hero try their luck!

SUPERMAN SAYS... This game is based on the old favourite, Simon Says.

Your superheroes each find a space in the room, and must follow your commands, such as 'Superman says... bend an iron bar!' or 'Superman says... leap a tall building in a single bound!'

To try to trick the players, add a few commands that superheroes would never do, like 'Superman says... iron your underpants!', and 'Superman says... play with a teddy bear!' The players must ignore these silly orders.

There are no winners or losers in this game, just lots of fun and giggles as everyone tries to work out what a superhero would and wouldn't do!

Here are a few serious commands to use:

◆ Fly around the world!
◆ Blow out a fire!
◆ Rescue a kitten from up a tree!
◆ Stop a runaway bus!
◆ Tie up ten bad guys!

And a few not so serious:

◆ Cry because you're lost!
◆ Skip around the room!
◆ Dress up your dolls!
◆ Bake a cake!
◆ Put ribbons in your hair!

SECRET IDENTITY. Clark Kent is Superman, Peter Parker is Spiderman, and Bruce Wayne is Batman. As mentioned earlier, every superhero has a secret identity – but can your guests guess who theirs is in this great game?

Write the name of a famous person, either real or fictional, on a piece of card for each guest. Then, without telling them who they are, pin a name onto everyone's back.

When the game starts, players must ask each other questions to try to guess who they really are – but they can only ask questions that can be answered with a 'yes' or a 'no'.

So, they could ask 'Am I a man?', 'Am I a film star?' or 'Am I from a book?' Each 'yes' or 'no' answer should give them a clue to who they are when not fighting crime.

When they think they know, they should come up to you to guess. If they're right, they win 10 points. If not, they must go back and ask more questions.

Keep playing until everyone has guessed their identity, and don't forget to give out a few hints to anyone who is really stuck!

food

You can provide your guests with superhero sandwiches, and crime fighting crisps – but here are a few suggestions for more unique ideas...

KRYPTONITE. The only thing that causes Superman to lose his powers – and there's loads of the stuff around. The only way that your superhero guests can save him is to get rid of the stuff – by eating it!

In reality, they're eating green fizzy jelly – but don't tell them that! Simply make a bowl of jelly as normal, but substitute some of the water with a can of lemonade. When the jelly is cool, but before it sets, pour it into waterproof sandwich bags, and tie the tops. Stick a 'Danger! Kryptonite!' label on the side of each bag, and leave them in the fridge to set.

POWERADE! A secret formula, created especially for this party, that increases each of your superhero's powers after they have drunk it.

To make it, pour out glasses of clear lemonade, and let each guest choose a Powerade cube from a bowl. When they drop the cube into the lemonade, the drink will change colour, releasing the cube's secret powers!

To make Powerade cubes, add a drop of food colouring to the water in ice cube trays, and let them set in the freezer. Make a few trays with different colours, and let each superhero choose their own from a bowl.

Party Bags

When the bad guys have been dealt with, hand out bags for your superheroes to hide their costumes in as they return to their secret identities and go home. Include a couple of superhero comics, and trading cards for your guests to enjoy until the day needs saving again!

Have a SUPER party!

Toon Time

**Run as fast as Speedy Gonzalez to a party where you can
eat like Taz and have more laughs than Daffy Duck!**

Invitations

Create your own comic strip to invite guests to a party crammed with cartoon capers! Don't worry if you can't draw very well – it's only there to get some information across.

Start by working out who your character will be. If it's a birthday party, make the hero your birthday child!

Draw the first panel (one square of a comic strip) with the character looking bored. In the next panel, have an adult stick their head into the frame saying, 'Let's have a party!' From then on, each successive panel should give out a new detail within the speech bubbles: where the party is, what date and time, and how long it will last. Draw each of these panels in pencil so that you can correct any mistakes, and make it all as big, clear and simple as possible. Have someone else read the comic to see if they can understand what you're trying to say. If they can't, make the necessary changes now.

When you're happy with your cartoon, it's time to 'ink'. Starting with the words (as they're the most important part), carefully draw over your pencil lines with a new, black felt pen. After you've completed the first frame, lay a sheet of clean paper over it to stop you from accidentally smudging the ink as you move on.

When the comic strip is finished, photocopy one for each of your guests, and hand them out.

Decoration

You're going to turn your party room into Toon Town!

Draw popular cartoon characters onto large sheets of card, paint them, and cut them out. This is a little more tricky than the comic strip invites so, if you're not confident of doing a good job yourself, find someone with a little artistic ability to help.

Stick these cartoon heroes all around the walls. You could have Tom chasing Jerry, Fred Flintstone fighting off Dino's kisses, or even Dexter working in his laboratory.

You don't have to limit yourself to characters for the walls. How about hanging the three Powerpuff Girls from the ceiling with cotton? Or having Bugs Bunny emerging from a black, cardboard hole in the floor? (If you're not sure who some of these cartoon characters are - ask your kids!)

Paint an empty cardboard box black, add '100 kg' in white along the side, and hang it over the doorway!

Finally, if you have a TV and video recorder, play a tape of cartoons with the volume turned down.

Costumes

In your comic strip invites, ask your guests to come dressed as their favourite animated characters. This is easier than you might think...

A large hat with piece of cloth pinned to the side looks like a deerstalker. Add a cardboard rifle, and you've got Elmer Fudd. A little hair gel to create some spikes, yellow face paint and a skateboard produce an instant Bart Simpson. And a simple black t-shirt, pair of jeans and quiffed hair is all that is needed to produce my favourite character, Johnny Bravo.

Let your imagination run riot!

Games

Time to get animated with these great game ideas, perfect for cartoon crazy kids!

CATCH THE ROADRUNNER! This one is just plain silly. I giggled like mad when I played it (yes, I test all these games out myself!).

Blow up as many balloons as your breath will let you – but don't tie any knots in them. You can stop them from deflating by pinching the necks with strong clothes pegs, or by cutting narrow slits into the edge of a piece of card, and carefully pushing the balloon necks into them. Use a marker pen to draw a simple cartoon of the Roadrunner's face on each balloon.

Your party guests find themselves a space somewhere in the room, and get ready to catch (this game works even better if you can play it outside in the garden!).

Simply hold the mouth of a balloon between your finger and thumb, and release.

The aim of the game is for one of the players to catch the Roadrunner before he hits the floor! It's chaos as soon as you let go of the balloon as nobody knows which direction it will fly in. If anyone manages to catch it, award them ten points. *(Remind older players to watch out for smaller kids around them so that no-one gets hurt.)*

Keep releasing balloons until they're all gone and, for extra fun, let go of two or more at the same time!

I'm giggling again now; I'm going to get my balloons...!

ACTING ANIMATED. Split your party guests into groups of three or four, depending on how many there are. They have five minutes to go to a corner of the room and work out a one minute cartoon, based on all their characters.

It doesn't matter if it doesn't make sense – when did you last see a realistic cartoon? Remind them how long they have left at regular intervals.

When the time is up, everyone should sit in their groups around the edges of the room. Choose the first group to come forward, and act out their cartoon. If you have a cartoon on video that has a minute of music without any dialogue, record it onto tape, and play it in the background as they perform.

When the cartoon is over, encourage everyone to applaud and cheer, then ask the next group to show their tiny 'toon.

It's animated anarchy!

SKETCHY DETAILS. For this game you'll need a large flipchart with blank pages, either standing on an easel, or on a table, resting against the wall. You'll also require a few thick marker pens. Prior to the party, prepare a set of cards with cartoon characters' names on. Try to have around twice as many cards as guests.

Split the guests into two teams, and get them to sit on the floor, facing the flipchart. To play the game, one player steps froward from the first team, and is given the first card in the pile – but they must not show it to anyone else. They now have one and a half minutes to draw that cartoon character on the flipchart in front of them.

The remaining players on both teams must shout out and try to guess who the character is. The first person to call out correctly wins ten points for their team.

Explain a few basic rules to the players before they start:

◆ They are not allowed to speak while they are drawing.
◆ They cannot write any words on the paper.
◆ If they don't know who the character is, they can choose another card before they start.

Remember that they don't have to draw the exact character – any combination of sketches that produces a correct guess will do. For example, instead of drawing Spiderman himself, a player could draw a spider next to a man. Or three heads could signify Ed, Edd and Eddy.

When a character is correctly guessed, or the time is up, a player from the opposite team steps forward to choose a card. Keep playing until everyone has had a couple of turns at sketching.

Food

In cartoons, the food mainly consists of Tweety Pie in a sandwich – so try these tastier 'toon treats...

COW PIE! Desperate Dan's favourite! However, if your guests aren't keen on pies, you can create the same effect with cakes. Simply cut two horn shapes from card for each cake, stick them onto wooden kebab sticks, and push them into the top of the cakes. Remind everyone to remove them before eating!

BANGERS AND MASH. The traditional feast at the end of a successful cartoon, and it's amazingly easy to make! A huge pile of mashed potato (instant mash works best here), with sausages sticking out at irregular intervals. Serve on your largest plate, and let your guests tuck in!

Party Bags

Make your own party bags by covering plain paper bags with pages from comics, or the 'funnies' section of the Sunday newspaper.

Fill the bags with comics, small sketchpads, and a packet of felt pens to encourage your guests to draw their own comic strips after the party is over.

That's all folks!

Who Wants to be a Millionaire?

**Phone your friends and invite them to this party
based on the popular TV quiz show!**

Invitations

Write invites to this millionaire mayhem on the back of fake cheques. On a PC, create a £1million cheque from the Boredom Busters Bank, and make it payable to your party guest. On the reverse of the cheque, add the 'small print' that the cheque is not real, and that the payee must attend the party at the specific date and time.

Decoration

Time to recreate the set for the famous TV quiz – and a little more!

Cover the walls of your party room with logos from the show (you can copy these onto paper from the web site at *www.itv.com/millionaire*), and make over-sized cheques for £1million to stick up alongside them.

Place chairs around the outside of the room, and the two seats facing each other in the centre for the contestant and show host.

For added effect, record the 'new question' incidental music onto tape to play during the quiz – or simply get your party guests to sing it out loud!

Costumes

While there may not be obvious costumes to wear to this party – there is a built in opportunity for fun!

One of the lifelines available during the show gives contestants the chance to 'phone a friend'. Well, at your party – guests also have the chance to 'BE a friend'!

On your invites, ask your guests to come dressed as one of their friends – preferably, one of the other party guests! They'll have great fun imitating their school friends' clothing, hairstyles and mannerisms. For added fun, see if your guests can work out who their friends are supposed to be!

Games

Play these crazy currency contests before ending the games session with the Millionaire quiz itself...

FUNNY MONEY! A whiz around the world game to match cash with country.

Make two identical wall charts on sheets of card listing ten different countries, such as France, America, Japan, etc. Then make two sets of cards with the names of currencies that match the countries – Euro, Dollars, Yen... Attach double sided tape to the backs of these cards, and lay them face down on two separate tables. Check with the currency exchange board at your local bank for a suitable list.

Split your party guests into two teams and, when the game starts, the first player from each team must grab a card at random from their table, and try to match it with the respective country on their wall chart.

As soon as they have stuck the card next to one of the countries, they sit back down, and the next player from each team jumps up to play. They can either grab a new card or, if they think the first player has made a mistake, move the card to a new country.

Play continues with each consecutive player either placing a new card or moving an existing one (their team mates can, of course, shout out their encouragement) until all the cards have been stuck onto the chart.

Mark the teams by giving one point for each correct match. The team with the highest score wins!

WHAT'S IT WORTH? Another team game where players have to guess at the value of various items to win points.

Cut pictures of household items, toys, food, etc from magazines or catalogues, and stick them onto index cards. On the back of each card, write the price of the item, as listed in the magazine. Give each team several sheets of paper and a marker pen, and you're ready to play.

Hold up the picture cards in turn, and tell the teams what each item is. The players then have 30 seconds to confer and guess what the item costs and write it down. When the time is up, the teams hold up their sheets of paper, and you flip over the card to reveal the answer. The team closest to the actual price wins one point or, of they guess the cost exactly, award them two points.

When you have exhausted your supply of cards, add up the points to see which team wins!

WHO WANTS TO BE A MILLIONAIRE? The quiz itself!

Seat your party guests in the chairs around the edge of the room, and set up the two seats in the centre.

Invite the first guest up to sit opposite you, and explain the rules of the game. You will ask 15 questions with four possible answers which will, if answered correctly, win £1million! *(This would probably be a good point to offer a short disclaimer in case there are any budding lawyers in the room! They are playing to **pretend** to win £1million!)*

Each player can, if they need help, use three lifelines:

◆ Phone a friend. *The player can choose a friend from the room to help them.*
◆ 50/50. *Remove two of the wrong answers, and leave the right answer and one wrong answer.*

◆ Ask the audience. *Invite the rest of the party guests to guess at the answer with a show of hands.*

Each lifeline can only be used once.

To prepare the questions, buy a kids' quiz book, and write out the questions you want to use on a sheet of paper, mixing the right answer in with three wrong ones. For the easier questions, make the wrong answers very obvious and as funny as possible.

Get one of the other guests to help you keep score for the contestants. After each correctly answered question, the players 'win' the following amounts:

◆ £100
◆ £200
◆ £300
◆ £500
◆ £1,000
◆ £2,000
◆ £4,000
◆ £8,000
◆ £16,000
◆ £32,000
◆ £64,000
◆ £125,000
◆ £250,000
◆ £500,000
◆ £1million

If a contestant answers a question incorrectly, their turn ends and they have to take their seat back with the 'audience'.

To keep any guests who are not currently playing from getting bored (and to stop them from whispering out the answers!), give them each a pad and a pen to write as many of the answers to the questions as they can – the audience member with the highest number of correct answers will win a consolation prize!

When each of your party guests have had a turn on the hot seat, ask your score keeper to tell you which player came closest to the £1million. Whoever it is gets the grand prize! While you won't be giving out a large cheque (we don't want to give you that!), a good prize would be the Who Wants To Be A Millionaire CD-ROM, or board game. For the highest scorer in the audience, why not give a book token?

Food

With big money games, you need big money grub! Try these ideas to satisfy expensive tastes...

CUCUMBER SANDWICHES. The garden party classic! But you could spice yours up by smothering them in salad cream!

MILLIONAIRE MOUSSE. Rich chocolate mousse, with pieces of real chocolate mixed in. Cover with chocolate sprinkles, and serve with chocolate ice cream, and chocolate chip cookies!

Party Bags

As they say on quiz shows, no-one goes home empty handed! Give your guests a party bag containing a wallet, quiz book, and a bag of chocolate coins!

Now that's rich!